WHAT YOUR MIND NEEDS FOR ANXIOUS MOMENTS

A 60-Day Guide to Take Control
of Your Thoughts

HOLLEY GERTH

Revell
a division of Baker Publishing Group
Grand Rapids, Michigan

© 2022 by Holley, Inc

Published by Revell
a division of Baker Publishing Group
PO Box 6287, Grand Rapids, MI 49516-6287
www.revellbooks.com

Printed in the United States of America

Library of Congress Cataloging-in-Publication Data
Names: Gerth, Holley, author.
Title: What your mind needs for anxious moments : a 60-day guide to take control of your thoughts / Holley Gerth.
Description: Grand Rapids, MI : Revell, a division of Baker Publishing Group, [2022]
Identifiers: LCCN 2021058173 | ISBN 9780800738549 (cloth) | ISBN 9781493438808 (ebook)
Subjects: LCSH: Thought and thinking—Religious aspects—Christianity. | Anxiety—Religious aspects—Christianity. | Bible—Meditations. | Devotional literature.
Classification: LCC BV4598.4 .G48 2022 | DDC 152.4/6—dc23/eng/20220128
LC record available at https://lccn.loc.gov/2021058173

Baker Publishing Group publications use paper produced from sustainable forestry practices and post-consumer waste whenever possible.

22 23 24 25 26 27 28   7 6 5 4 3 2 1

OTHER WORKS BY HOLLEY GERTH

You're Already Amazing
You're Made for a God-Sized Dream
You're Going to Be Okay
What Your Heart Needs for the Hard Days
You're Loved No Matter What
Fiercehearted
Hope Your Heart Needs
Strong, Brave, Loved
The Powerful Purpose of Introverts
What Your Soul Needs for Stressful Times

WHAT YOUR MIND NEEDS
FOR ANXIOUS MOMENTS

CONTENTS

INTRODUCTION

We all have anxious thoughts. Maybe yours happen when you watch the news, worry about a loved one, get ready for a big meeting, or stare at the ceiling in the night worrying about the future. Your heart might pound, your mind may race, or your sleep could get interrupted.

Your anxiety might even make you wonder if your faith is weak or something is wrong with you. But neither of those are true. Anxiety is an inevitable part of being human, but it doesn't have to control your mind. You really can live with more contentment and less worry, more inner peace and less fear, more joy and less stress.

How do I know? Because one in every five Americans has anxiety significant enough to be diagnosed with a disorder, and I'm among them. A recent poll showed

62 percent of people feel more anxious than they did a year ago.[1] We've had a lot to deal with in recent history, including global issues like the pandemic, divisive politics, and personal obstacles we never expected.

While we're facing new challenges, anxiety itself is as old as humanity. Adam and Eve hid in the garden because they were anxious. Peter experienced anxiety when he tried to walk on water but found himself sinking. Paul encouraged the Philippians not to be anxious but to take every detail of their lives to God. This book will guide you on a journey from Genesis to Revelation, focusing on times when biblical characters experienced anxiety. We'll explore what God wants to show us through those stories so you can apply these lessons to your life.

As a counselor and life coach, as well as someone who has personally struggled with anxiety, I understand its challenges and what actually helps. *What Your Mind Needs for the Anxious Moments* shares what I've learned, along with brain science, psychological insights, and practical steps. If you've ever been frustrated because you felt anxious and someone told you, "Just pray about it," then this little book is especially for you. God created us as beings with a mind, heart, body, and soul. To overcome our anxiety, we need support in *all* those areas.

You don't have to keep putting up with your anxiety.

You don't have to stay stuck in the same old worries.

You don't have to continue surrendering your joy to stress.

This is the divine invitation offered to you: "Throw all your anxiety onto him, because he cares about you" (1 Pet. 5:7 CEB). God alone is big enough to carry your burdens, work out all your worries, and take your anxious moments and transform them into soul-deep peace. His love for you is endless, his grace complete, and his plan for your life full of hope. He alone can set you free from anxiety one moment, one thought, one step at a time—starting right now.

For more tools and resources to help with your anxiety as you go through this guide, visit www.holleygerth.com/anxiety.

ONE

God Will Meet You Where You Are Today

Then the LORD God called to the man, "Where are you?"
He replied, "I heard you walking in the garden, so I hid.
I was afraid because I was naked."

Genesis 3:9–10

Imagine the most beautiful place you've ever visited. Maybe you watched the sunset at a beach and recall the sky aflame with orange and red, the rhythm of the waves, the smell of salt. Perhaps you stood at the edge of the Grand Canyon or on the peak of a mountain, the rugged landscape reminding you that God is big and you are small. Whatever comes to mind, it cannot even compare to Eden.

There God gives Adam and Eve everything they need, all they want. But the serpent's question, "Did God really say . . . ?" (Gen. 3:1) introduces a seed of

13

doubt. It grows until Eve takes a bite of the forbidden fruit and Adam, who is with her, follows suit.

In an instant, everything changes. Innocence turns to shame, peace gives way to fear, joy is distorted into despair. For the first time, humanity feels *anxious*. Anxiety is defined as "a feeling of worry, nervousness, or unease, typically about an imminent event or something with an uncertain outcome."[1] Here, the unknown event is what will happen next, what God will do.

In his great tenderness, what God does is go looking for Adam and Eve. He asks a question, "Where are you?" Adam responds, "I heard you walking in the garden, so I hid. I was afraid because I was naked" (vv. 9–10).

We've been responding in similar ways ever since. Anxiety still tells us we have to hide. We may not do so physically, but we hide emotionally. We pretend we're okay. We're fine, just fine. We hold it together on the outside while on the inside we're falling apart.

Adam and Eve experienced anxiety because of a rebellious choice. But most of us don't *choose* to have anxiety. When, at age eight, I started having stomachaches and visiting the nurse's office almost every day at school, I didn't invite anxiety into my life. It simply showed up, an unwanted visitor who refused to leave. Maybe anxiety has been with you for years, like it has for me. The tendency to be anxious is wired into our human biology as surely as the color of our eyes. Maybe anxiety is new for you. You've recently been through a challenge or a trauma. Or the news headlines have just become too much to handle.

Whatever the source of our anxiety, if we've been told it's bad or wrong to be anxious, then it can lead to another uncomfortable feeling that makes us want to hide—shame. Shame tells us that something must be wrong with us if we're struggling with anxiety or that we're the only ones who do. But neither are true (we'll talk a lot more about this as we go forward).

Author and researcher Brené Brown says, "Shame hates it when we reach out and tell our story. It hates having words wrapped around it—it can't survive being shared. Shame loves secrecy. The most dangerous thing to do after a shaming experience is hide or bury our story."[2] God goes looking for us because he doesn't want us to stay in our shame. He wants to not only hear about our anxiety but also be in it with us because he's relentlessly for us.

In my life, God has used many forms of healing to help with my anxiety, including prayer, counseling, working with my doctor, changing habits in my daily life, talking to supportive people, and even understanding the brain science behind my anxiety. On our journey in this book, I'll share more about all those with you. But they all began when I found the courage to admit my struggle.

God is asking you today, "Where are you?" No matter the answer, he already knows. What he's really asking is, "Are you ready to let me meet you where you are today?" God wants to free you from shame, deliver you from fear, and bring you to a new place of overcoming your anxiety. He's calling to your heart, even now. He loves you even in your most anxious moments. It's time to come out of hiding.

· ·

God, thank you for your great tenderness toward me. I'm so grateful you want to meet me where I am today. I need your help with my anxiety. Amen.

What's one way you'd like God to help you with your anxiety?

TWO

God Sees Everything in Your Life

> But God heard the boy crying, and the angel of God called to
> Hagar from heaven, "Hagar, what's wrong? Do not be afraid!"
>
> Genesis 21:17

What if something bad happens to someone I love? It's an anxiety-provoking question, and one Hagar faces in the desert. The Egyptian servant of Abraham, she bore him a son when his wife, Sarah, couldn't conceive. Thankfully, this isn't a practice we continue today, nor is it one God approves of, but it was common in the ancient world.

All goes well for Hagar until years later, when Sarah has a son of her own. Like so many siblings, Ishmael makes fun of his little brother. The consequences are worse than being grounded or sent to his room. Sarah demands that Hagar and Ishmael leave.

Hagar wanders in the desert, not knowing where to go or how she'll take care of her son. When her water is gone, she places Ishmael in the only bit of shade she can find. She sits down a short distance away and cries. As she likely did in so many other moments of her life, Hagar feels powerless. "But God *heard the boy crying*, and the angel of God called to Hagar from heaven, 'Hagar, what's wrong? Do not be afraid!'" (Gen. 21:17, emphasis added). It's interesting this verse doesn't say, "God heard Hagar crying." He knows Hagar's tears aren't her greatest concern; instead, it's the pain of her son.

When we're anxious about those we love, it feels as if their well-being depends on us. We have to keep them safe. We have to ensure they make the right choices. We need to control what happens. But the story of Hagar and Ishmael reminds us that God is ultimately in charge of those we love. He is their Protector. He is their Provider. He is the one who will meet them in the dry, desert places where there seems to be no hope.

God reassures Hagar that he has a plan for Ishmael's life. Then he tells her, "Go to him and comfort him" (v. 18). We can't determine the future of those we love. We can't make every problem go away. We can't prevent them from ever experiencing pain. But we can be a loving, supportive presence in their lives.

As Hagar listens to God, her perspective shifts. Then God opens Hagar's eyes. She sees a well full of water, quickly fills her water container, and gives the boy a drink. From a human viewpoint, there is no way out of this situation. But when Hagar sees circumstances as God does, everything changes.

When we find ourselves anxious about someone we love, we can take our concerns to God. Then we can comfort, encourage, and be there for that person. We can't control the results of the situation, but we can choose how we will be present in the relationship. Worrying can't change what will happen, but prayerfully walking with someone through whatever comes their way can make all the difference.

....

God, thank you for loving the people in my life even more than I do. I'm especially concerned about _____. Please take care of this person today in ways only you can. Amen.

When have you seen God take care of someone you love?

THREE

God's Love and Promises Are Real

Live here as a foreigner in this land, and I will be with you and bless you.

Genesis 26:3

Isaac thinks of when he first met his wife, Rebekah, how her beauty took his breath away, and her comforting companionship took his grief for his mother away too. What would he do without her?

To survive a famine, they'd recently moved to the Philistine territory of Gerar. At first Isaac felt uneasy in this foreign land, but the Lord appeared to him and said he would be blessed and prosperous there, that this land would one day belong to Isaac and his descendants. The covenant God made with his father, Abraham, would continue with him.

Then this morning in the market a group of Philistine men asked about Rebekah. "Who is that beautiful woman we see with you?" A scene flashed through Isaac's mind—these men kicking in the door of his home, the feel of a knife in his side as he watched his beloved Rebekah dragged into the night. "She is my sister," he said (Gen. 26:7).

Remembering that conversation, Isaac reaches protectively for his wife. "Isaac, what's gotten into you?" Rebekah asks as she hugs him. It feels like a private moment, but King Abimelech sees the two of them embrace, calls for Isaac, and exclaims, "She is obviously your wife! Why did you say, 'She is my sister'?" (v. 9). Isaac answers, "Because I was afraid someone would kill me to get her from me" (v. 9).

When God told Isaac he would bless him in this land, Isaac believed and obeyed. But in this one area of his life, fear still has a stronghold. So Isaac creates an image that doesn't align with truth.

Isaac isn't the first in his family to do so. His father, Abraham, did the exact same thing. "While living there as a foreigner, Abraham introduced his wife, Sarah, by saying, 'She is my sister.' So King Abimelech of Gerar sent for Sarah and had her brought to him at his palace" (20:1–2). God intervened before Abimelech touched Sarah, but it was almost a disaster, and surely Isaac knew this story.

Sometimes the image we take on is passed from one generation to another. Anxiety whispered to Abraham, then Isaac, "If people really knew who your 'sister' is . . ." But for us today, what we're more likely to hear from anxiety is, "If people really knew who *you* are . . ."

You wouldn't be loved.

You'd never be accepted.

You'd be alone and rejected.

So we act like everything is fine, overachieve to prove our worth, overspend to keep up with our neighbors, or simply never dare to let ourselves be deeply known.

How do we stop repeating these patterns? *We return to the truth.* Abraham and Isaac did so because they were forced. But we can choose to do so as an act of faith. In our everyday lives, that might look like showing up as we are, not as the person we sometimes pretend to be; asking for help even though it makes us feel vulnerable; and remembering we don't have to cultivate an image to impress people, because we were created in the image of God.

God spoke promises to Isaac, and he speaks promises to you too.

You are already loved.

You are already accepted.

He will never leave or forsake you.

Anxiety says we have to pretend, but God invites us to entrust our real, imperfect, in-progress selves to him.

. . . .

God, when anxiety tempts me to portray an image to the world, remind me that I'm loved, I'm accepted, and you are with me always. You get the final word in my life, and what you speak is always true. Amen.

What's one area of your life in which you feel pressure to create an image? What helps you return to the truth of who God made you?

FOUR

God Is Working on Your Behalf

You intended to harm me, but God intended it all for good.

Genesis 50:20

Family dysfunction, false accusations, wrongful imprisonment—Joseph's life is filled with one anxiety-provoking situation after another. Joseph is his father's favored son, so his brothers sell him to traders out of jealousy. Joseph ends up in the house of Potiphar, an official of Pharaoh. Just when things look better, Potiphar's wife tries to seduce Joseph. He refuses her advances and she frames him for rape. Stuck in prison, it seems Joseph's luck has run out.

Then Pharaoh has a dream no one can explain, and his cupbearer remembers Joseph interpreted a dream for him while they were in prison together. Pharaoh summons Joseph, who tells him the dream depicts seven years of plenty followed by seven years of famine. Pharaoh is so impressed with Joseph that he puts him in charge of Egypt.

Years later, the brothers who sold Joseph arrive to buy food, but they don't recognize their long-lost sibling until he reveals himself to them. Reunited with his family, Joseph says, "You intended to harm me, but God intended it all for good" (Gen. 50:20).

When we experience hard circumstances, anxiety tries to lie to us. It tells us, "Things are bad, and they're only going to get worse." Maybe anxiety whispers, "You can't handle this." Or it accuses us, "If your faith was stronger, then you wouldn't be going through this right now." Joseph certainly had reason to believe these lies. He could have listened to anxiety and become hopeless. Instead, he chose to see God's hand even in the most difficult places.

Pause and ask yourself, "What does anxiety try to tell me?" We each have signature lies directed at the most tender parts of who we are. In my life, anxiety tries to tell me, "You're not good enough." I worry I've messed everything up or let God down. But there's a flaw in this kind of thinking; it assumes that if I follow God, then all will go well. Jesus tells us, "Here on earth you will have many trials and sorrows" (John 16:33). In this world, we will experience heartbreak, failure, disappointment, and loss. This doesn't mean we've done something wrong; it simply means we are not in heaven yet.

Jesus goes on to say, "But take heart, because I have overcome the world" (v. 33). Although Joseph lived long before Jesus, we still see this truth in his life. Joseph took heart by continuing to trust God was at work even when all the outward evidence seemed to indicate otherwise. He saw beyond what was possible from a human perspective and believed God would get him through whatever came.

When anxiety tries to lie to us, we can do the same by turning to the truth.

Anxiety says, "Things are bad and going to get worse."

Truth says, "God causes everything to work together for the good of those who love God and are called according to his purpose for them" (Rom. 8:28).

Anxiety says, "You can't handle this."

Truth says, "I can do everything through Christ, who gives me strength" (Phil. 4:13).

Anxiety says, "If your faith was stronger, then you wouldn't be going through this right now."

Truth says,

> When you go through deep waters,
> I will be with you.

> When you go through rivers of difficulty,
>   you will not drown.
> When you walk through the fire of oppression,
>   you will not be burned up;
>   the flames will not consume you. (Isa. 43:2)

Because Joseph persevered, God used him to save the lives of thousands of people, including his family. What seemed like pointless pain served a greater purpose. Whatever you're going through today, whatever anxiety is trying to say, God is still working in your life. Even when you can't yet see his hand, he's accomplishing his good plan to give you hope and a future.

God, thank you for working all things together for good in my life. When anxiety tries to lie to me, help me hold on to truth and remember how much you love me. Amen.

What's a hard circumstance in your life that God used for good?

FIVE

God Will Make a Way for You

Don't be afraid. Just stand still and watch the LORD rescue you today. . . . The LORD himself will fight for you. Just stay calm.

Exodus 14:13–14

The people of Israel are free. After years of slavery, God has delivered them from the Egyptians through Moses. Men slap each other on the back in congratulations. Women smile as they walk, holding their children's hands. Their sons and daughters will grow up without the burden of serving a foreign land. Then God gives a strange command through Moses: turn back.

The people are confused as they retreat and set up camp. Then they hear an unmistakable sound in the distance—chariot wheels. The Egyptian army has come for them. Prayers slip from the lips of mothers. Frowns overtake the faces of fathers. Children look for hiding places.

How could this be happening? Their anxiety spills out as accusatory questions to Moses: "Why did you bring us out here to die in the wilderness? Weren't there enough graves for us in Egypt? What have you done to us? Why did you make us leave Egypt?" (Exod. 14:11).

In this moment, their leader doesn't offer practical answers. He doesn't defend his decision, even though God has already told Moses the victorious outcome. He also doesn't condemn the Israelites. Instead, he speaks to them as a parent would to a terrified child. Moses tells the people, "Don't be afraid. Just stand still and watch the LORD rescue you today. The Egyptians you see today will never be seen again. The LORD himself will fight for you. Just stay calm" (vv. 13–14).

When anxiety tries to overcome us, it can feel much like it did for the Israelites. We look at overwhelming circumstances, and suddenly questions come to our minds. "Why is this happening to me? What have I gotten myself into? I should have seen this coming!" In those moments, we can follow Moses's example.

First, he acknowledges the fear the Israelites are experiencing. We can pause and recognize that fear is at the root of our response too. Then instead of telling the people what to do, he invites the people to slow down. "Stand still and watch," he tells them. We can also take a deep breath and look at what's really going on around us.

Then Moses offers truth—the Lord will rescue the people. We can also speak truth to our anxious hearts. Moses reminds the people that this battle is not theirs to win. "The Lord himself will fight for you," he says. "Just stay calm." Our battles are not our own either. We can trust that God is fighting for us in whatever we face.

Then God tells Moses to instruct the people to get going, which is interesting because he has just finished telling them to stand still. We can be still on the inside while taking helpful, obedient action on the outside. When we're anxious, we can slow down, calm ourselves, and then ask, "What's one small step I can take?"

Most of us have heard the story of what happens next. God parts the waters of the Red Sea and the Israelites walk through it. The outcome in our lives might not be as dramatic, but the truth of this story is the same: God will make a way. He will lead us out of anxiety and into peace. He will guide us beyond fear and into courage. He will replace our questions with the certainty of his unfailing love.

....

God, nothing is too difficult for you. No circum-stance is too challenging, no obstacle too big, no situation beyond your solutions. When anxiety leads me to question the future, help me trust that you are working in ways beyond what I can even imagine. Amen.

Try going through the process Moses used with a situation that causes anxiety in your life.

1. Acknowledge your fear.
2. Slow down and take a deep breath.
3. Speak truth to your anxious heart.
4. Remember that the battle isn't yours.
5. Take one small step of obedience.

SIX

God Gives You a New Song

I will sing to the LORD,
   for he has triumphed gloriously;
he has hurled both horse and rider
   into the sea.
The LORD is my strength and my song;
   he has given me victory.

Exodus 15:1–2

Standing on the other side of the Red Sea, safe from danger, Moses and the Israelites do more than breathe a sigh of relief; they *sing*. It's the first song ever recorded in the Bible, a spontaneous, communal response that comes from a deep awe of God. It was an act of worship, and modern scientists have discovered that it also helped restore their sense of well-being after their stressful experience.

When I look at the discoveries made about our brains and nervous systems, I feel a sense of awe too. Only God could create every part of us so perfectly, giving us everything we need to not just survive but thrive. It turns out that when we sing, it stimulates and strengthens our vagus nerve. Counselors Yana Hoffman and Dr. Hank Davis explain, "The 'wandering' or vagus nerve is the longest cranial nerve in the body. It connects the brain and the gut, lungs, and heart. And it plays a critical role in helping us 'rest and digest.' Increasing the tone of the vagus nerve enables our body to relax faster after experiencing stress."[1]

Singing can not only help us recover from stress but also give us more courage and holy calm in anxiety-provoking situations. King Jehoshaphat receives news that enemy armies will soon attack his people. When his troops go to fight, the king appoints "singers to walk ahead of the army, singing to the Lord and praising him for his holy splendor. This is what they sang: 'Give thanks to the Lord; his faithful love endures forever!'" (2 Chron. 20:21).

As the worshipers sing, God causes the enemy armies to become confused, leading to victory for Israel.

You don't need to be a musician to get the physical and spiritual benefits of singing. I'm a terrible singer.

I've even been known to mouth the words to songs in church to spare those around me (don't tell). My version of using singing to help with anxiety looks like turning on my favorite tunes as I get ready in the morning and sometimes singing along. I listen to music when I run and might join in if no one is around. Or if I'm driving to a meeting or event that makes me nervous, I occasionally belt out some fear-fighting lyrics in the privacy of my car.

If that still feels like a stretch to you, then you can try humming or repeating a phrase like "I am loved." Anything that gets your vocal cords going will give you the vagus nerve benefits and help calm your heart, soul, and mind.

All throughout Scripture, people sing—in times of difficulty, joy, sorrow, victory, fear, and everything in between. We can join David in saying,

> He has given me a new song to sing,
>   a hymn of praise to our God.
> Many will see what he has done and be amazed.
>   They will put their trust in the Lord. (Ps. 40:3)

. . . .

God, you are the song of my heart, the focus of my worship, the one who causes words of praise

to rise up within me. Give me a new song to sing,
one of calm and courage. Amen.

What's one way you can use music to help manage your anxiety today?

SEVEN

God Can Handle Your Questions

The angel of the LORD appeared to him and said, "Mighty hero, the LORD is with you!"

Judges 6:12

Gideon hears a sound in the night and ducks into a dark corner. His heart pounds as he imagines a robber appearing, the last of his family's grain being stolen, the feel of a fist in his face. Then a sheep bleats, and he realizes it's only some wandering livestock looking for food, hungry just like Gideon and his family.

He steps out of the shadows and starts threshing wheat again. He's doing this chore in the bottom of a winepress, hoping to stay out of sight from the raiders who have been ravaging his country and pushing his people into poverty.

Just as his breathing slows down, Gideon hears another sound. This time an angel sent by God says, "Mighty hero, the Lord is with you!" (Judg. 6:12). It's a strange greeting, considering Gideon is hiding, and the response Gideon gives seems even stranger. He doesn't fall down in awe or ask what God wants him to do. Instead, he launches into a series of questions.

> If the Lord is with us, why has all this happened to us? And where are all the miracles our ancestors told us about? Didn't they say, "The Lord brought us up out of Egypt"? (v. 13)

Gideon also says God has abandoned his people and handed them over to their enemies, and he asks for a sign. Even when God, through the angel, says to him, "Go with the strength you have, and rescue Israel from the Midianites. I am sending you!" (v. 14), Gideon responds with, "But Lord . . ." (v. 15).

So God zaps Gideon with a lightning bolt and picks someone else. The end.

Thankfully, that's not the way it goes. Instead, God does something interesting with anxious Gideon. He doesn't explain or defend himself. Instead, he keeps using "I" statements.

I am sending you! (v. 14)

I will be with you. (v. 16)

I will stay here until you return. (v. 18)

God knows what Gideon needs most isn't information, it's knowing who he can trust even when there are no easy answers.

One of the biggest signs of anxiety is endless questioning. What if? How will this work out? Can I do this? We think our questions have to go away or be fully answered before God can use us. But the story of Gideon shows us God can handle our questions. What matters is that we take steps of obedience *even as we're still questioning*.

My granddaughter is almost four, and she constantly asks questions. I can't always answer in a way that makes sense to her, but she's also not in trouble for asking. What I want is not for her to never ask questions but for her to trust me. Gideon's questions seem to come not from a place of doubt but from discouragement and a desire to understand. He keeps asking, but he also keeps obeying.

When we find ourselves in a place of fear like Gideon, we can bring God our concerns, hurts, and worries, and the ways we wish things were different. He's a safe place for all our emotions and uncertainty. Then he says to us, as he did to Gideon, "Go with the strength you have" (v. 14). Why? Because the strength we have is *his* strength. We may always question what's going on around us, but we can also always trust the One who lives within us.

....

God, there is so much I don't understand. When I want to hide and uncertainty surrounds me, give me the strength and courage to do what you are asking of me anyway. I choose to trust you. Amen.

What's a question you're asking today? What does God say in his Word that reassures you (for example, "I will be with you," "I am for you," "I love you")?

EIGHT

God Still Has a Plan for You

May the LORD, the God of Israel, under whose wings you have come to take refuge, reward you fully for what you have done.

Ruth 2:12

Memories flash through Naomi's mind as she walks the streets of her hometown for the first time in many years. Her wedding day, walking to the market with her little boys, one on her hip and the other holding her hand. Her family left this place to escape a famine, but now her husband and sons are gone.

"Is it really Naomi?" a familiar, though long unheard, voice asks (Ruth 1:19). "Don't call me Naomi," she responds. "Instead, call me Mara, for the Almighty has made life very bitter for me" (v. 20). Naomi's widowed daughter-in-law, Ruth, places a hand on her shoulder.

Ruth, a foreigner and gentile, grew up in a pagan land. It appears she came to the Jewish faith through Naomi's son and now seems to have an inexplicable strength beneath her grief. She weeps as Naomi does but not without hope. She worries but also worships, has tough days and yet persists in putting one foot in front of the other. Naomi has become hard and bitter; Ruth inexplicably remains softhearted and open.

One day Ruth tells Naomi she plans to glean barley in the fields. Jewish law allows the poor to gather the extra barley so they won't go hungry. Ruth providentially ends up in the field of Boaz, a relative of Naomi's husband. He shows kindness to her and says, "I also know about everything you have done for your mother-in-law. . . . May the LORD, the God of Israel, under whose wings you have come to take refuge, reward you fully for what you have done" (2:11–12).

It's the start of an unexpected love story, one that ends with Ruth marrying Boaz and not only giving birth to the grandfather of King David but also becoming part of the Messiah's lineage. Naomi's family line will continue, and for the first time in many years, she dares to dream about the future again. When the women of the town come to see the baby, they say, "May he restore your youth and care for you in your old age. For he is the son of your daughter-in-law who loves you and has been better to you than seven sons!" (4:15).

My grandmother had polio at the age of twenty-nine, when she was the mother of two young girls. Her pastor came to visit her in the hospital and said, "This can make you bitter or better." She likes to say with a smile, "I chose better." She has spent the rest of her life in a wheelchair.

At first Naomi chose bitter. Ruth chose better. Naomi gave up hope. Ruth kept pushing forward. Naomi believed her life was over. Ruth trusted God still had a plan beyond what she could understand.

We're not Naomi *or* Ruth. We all find ourselves acting like each woman at one point or another. What matters is that we recognize when we're slipping into bitterness. In those moments, what we need most is a friend, family member, wise counselor, or other support person. I have a dear friend I sometimes text when I'm anxious and simply say, "I can't remember what's true today. Can you remind me?" Sometimes our roles are reversed—she's Naomi and I'm Ruth.

What matters is that we help each other not give up because God is always still working out an unseen plan, even when we don't understand. Anxiety tells us, "It's all over." But faith, and the Ruths in our lives, remind us, "God isn't finished with your story yet."

....

God, when it seems easier to choose bitter instead of better, give me the strength to keep trusting you have a plan beyond what I can understand. Give me the courage to reach out to a Ruth when I need to, and show me who needs me to be a Ruth to them as well. Amen.

Who's a Ruth in your life? This person can be someone in your personal life or a counselor, someone who's present now or whose past influence still gives you hope. And is there someone who needs you to be a Ruth to them?

NINE

God Will Defeat the Giants in Your Life

"Don't worry about this Philistine," David told Saul. "I'll go fight him!"

1 Samuel 17:32

The battle lines have been drawn, Israelites on one side and Philistines on the other. For forty days, a Philistine giant named Goliath has come out to taunt his enemies. "Why are you all coming out to fight?" he calls. "I am the Philistine champion, but you are only the servants of Saul" (1 Sam. 17:8). Rather than responding with courage, Saul and the Israelites are "terrified and deeply shaken" (v. 11). They not only have a huge warrior to deal with, but they also have a massive case of anxiety.

Does this situation sound familiar? We all know what it's like to encounter a "giant" in our lives. Maybe it's a challenge at work, in a personal relationship, or with an old habit. Each day we tell ourselves we're going to overcome it, but we remain stuck in fear. Instead of making progress, we stay in self-protection mode. So how do we break the cycle?

For the Israelites, everything changes when David shows up at the battlefield—and not even as a soldier. Instead, as the youngest of many sons, he's been watching over the family's flock of sheep. Now his dad has sent him to bring his brothers snacks. He's running errands, not intending to become a hero.

But David brings something with him that no one else has—a different perspective. Saul, the Israelites, and even Goliath see this as a human battle. But David views it as a spiritual one.

When Saul tells David he can't possibly win because he's only a boy, David replies, "The Lord . . . will rescue me" (v. 37).

When Goliath warns David that he's going to be defeated, David responds, "The Lord will conquer you" (v. 46).

After forty days of the Israelites believing the outcome is up to them, David declares, "This is the Lord's battle" (v. 47).

How does this apply to our anxiety? We can use the same phrases that David did.

When anxiety tells us, "You can't handle this," we can reply, "The Lord will rescue me."

When anxiety warns we're going to be defeated, we can respond, "The Lord will conquer the giants in my life."

When anxiety tempts us to believe it's all up to us, we can declare, "This is the Lord's battle."

Most of us are familiar with the outcome of the fight between David and Goliath. With only a sling and a small stone, David took down a giant. What seemed impossible from an earthly viewpoint became reality when approached with an eternal perspective. Anxiety can make us see only what's possible within our human limitations. But we, like David, can look beyond those limitations to what only God can do.

Anxiety says, "You can't."

Faith says, "God can."

Anxiety says, "You won't."

Faith says, "God will."

We are never in the battle alone—and that makes all the difference.

....

God, thank you that I never have to face anything without you. When anxiety tries to tell me the giant in my life is going to win, bring me back to the truth of who you are again. You will rescue me. You will conquer the giants in my life. This is your battle. Amen.

When you imagine something, it activates the same neurons in your brain that would be triggered if that event actually happened. For forty days, the Israelites imagined losing to Goliath. Only David imagined winning. What we mentally rehearse matters. If you've been imagining losing to your "giant," pause and picture God empowering you to win instead. What scene did you see in your mind?

TEN

God Will Care for You

> But Elijah said to her, "Don't be afraid! Go ahead and do
> just what you've said."
>
> 1 Kings 17:13

As a widow, she knows the pain of loss, and now she's fighting off the pangs of hunger. As she gathers sticks to make a fire, she thinks of her husband. "I wish you were here," she whispers, but only the wind answers. She's a single mom who is devoted to her son and has given everything to him, but it's not enough. Famine has ravaged the land, and she's preparing their final meal. Scenes of the days she longed to see in her child's life flash through her mind—the first stubble of manhood appearing on his face, his wedding day, the birth of his first child. She mourns not only for what has been but what will never be. *Where are you, God?* she wonders.

Just then, a man calls out to her, "Would you please bring me a little water in a cup?" (1 Kings 17:10). It's a small request, one she can actually fulfill. She turns to get the water, and he adds, "Bring me a bite of bread, too" (v. 11).

Perhaps it's the months of loneliness getting the best of her, but she tells this man the whole story. "I swear by the LORD your God that I don't have a single piece of bread in the house. And I have only a handful of flour left in the jar and a little cooking oil in the bottom of the jug. I was just gathering a few sticks to cook this last meal, and then my son and I will die" (v. 12).

She feels the anxiety like a heavy stone in her heart, weighing her down, stealing her dreams. The man notices it too. "Don't be afraid!" he says (v. 13). Then he tells her to do what she has said, but first make him a little bread. Then he adds the impossible: "For this is what the LORD, the God of Israel, says: There will always be flour and olive oil left in your containers until the time when the LORD sends rain and the crops grow again!" (v. 14).

Her fear tells her this is foolish. Give her last bit of food (and hope) to a stranger? She doesn't need anyone. She and her son did just fine until the famine came. But desperation and a nudge deep inside her win out. She does as the man, whom she now knows is the prophet Elijah, tells her. And "there was always enough flour and olive oil left in the containers, just as the LORD had promised" (v. 16).

In challenging times, anxiety tells us, "You have to take care of yourself." It feels like it's all up to us. We might not be facing a physical famine, but anxiety can bring on an emotional one. It can seem as if we're down to our last bit of courage, hope, and strength. Sometimes in that moment God may ask us to do something that makes no sense at all. He might send someone into our lives to serve. He may invite us to tell our hard, brave story. He could nudge us toward a step of obedience that seems crazy to our rational minds.

What will we choose? When we dare to trust, we can discover our own version of this story. Yours might sound like this: "There was always enough courage and strength left in her heart, just as the Lord had promised."

Anxiety is an emotion of scarcity. It whispers that there's not enough, that we can't survive this, that we've been abandoned to fate. But we serve a God of abundance. With him, there is always more grace, more love, more of whatever we need in any moment.

....

God, thank you for being the source of what my heart needs today. When anxiety tries to tell me there's not enough, remind me you are a God of abundance. I'm not on my own, trying to take care of everything myself. You are with and for me always. Amen.

What is anxiety telling you that you don't have enough of today? What does God want to give you that will meet that need?

ELEVEN

God Understands You're Human

Then the angel of the LORD came again and touched him and said, "Get up and eat some more, or the journey ahead will be too much for you."

1 Kings 19:7

After Elijah experienced the miracle with the widow you read about yesterday, he never doubted or felt anxious again. He lived with faith, courage, and strength for the rest of his days. That sounds great, doesn't it? There's only one problem—it isn't true.

Here's the real story: perhaps emboldened by seeing God's provision, Elijah goes to King Ahab (which could have meant instant, certain death for him). He tells the king to gather the people of Israel as well as 950 pagan prophets for a spiritual showdown. The rules are simple: The pagan prophets and Elijah each build an altar to the god they worship. Then they call down fire to burn up a sacrifice on that altar. Whoever's god responds, wins.

The prophets of Baal try to no avail. Elijah taunts them, then prays to God. "Immediately the fire of the Lord flashed down from heaven and burned up the young bull, the wood, the stones, and the dust. It even licked up all the water in the trench!" (1 Kings 18:38).

When Ahab gets home, he tells his wicked wife, Jezebel, about the defeat. She sends a death threat to Elijah, and after seeing the amazing power of what God can do, Elijah is "afraid" and flees "for his life" (19:3). Then he sits down under a tree and tells God he's done, just take him on home to heaven. Then he lies down and falls asleep.

This scene in Scripture is so endearingly *human*. Haven't we all had moments of irrational anxiety and exhaustion, *even when we've just seen God work in our lives*? God's response to this situation is so reassuring. He didn't rebuke Elijah; instead, he sent an angel with snacks and water while Elijah took a nap. God didn't reason with Elijah when he was physically depleted. He didn't offer clichés or tell him to get over it. Instead, because he created our bodies, God knows sometimes what we need when we're anxious is to pray, and other times it's to pause and deal with what's going on in our bodies.

Then Elijah "got up and ate and drank, and the food gave him enough strength to travel forty days and forty nights to Mount Sinai, the mountain of God" (v. 8). If you are exhausted, hungry, thirsty, or physically depleted in another way, *it's okay to deal with that first.* Often once we do so, our anxiety level will go down, and we'll be able to move forward like Elijah did. If not, at least we'll be in a better, more rested state to address our anxiety in whatever other ways are needed.

Yes, we are filled with the mighty, supernatural power of God—the same power that sent down fire from heaven and raised Jesus from the dead. But for now, that power dwells within a very human body. Sometimes the most spiritual thing we can do is have a snack and a glass of water, then take a nap.

....

God, I'm so grateful for your extraordinary compassion toward my humanity. Sometimes I'm so much harder on myself than you are. Help me be aware of not just what my soul needs but my body too. Thank you that every provision, whether spiritual or physical, is a gift from you. Amen.

Think about the last time you were physically depleted in a way that increased your anxiety and perhaps even caused you to think irrationally. Write at least three things (example: nap or snack) that would help your body the next time you experience that kind of depletion.

TWELVE

God Will Never Let You Battle Alone

"Don't be afraid!" Elisha told him. "For there are more on our side than on theirs!"

2 Kings 6:16

Startled by a noise, the prophet Elisha's servant wakes early and walks outside to investigate. Troops, horses, and chariots are everywhere. They've come to kill Elisha, and he won't be spared either. Turning to see Elisha behind him, he exclaims, "Oh, sir, what will we do now?" (2 Kings 6:15).

Elisha responds, "Don't be afraid! . . . For there are more on our side than on theirs!" (v. 16). The servant looks around for his rescuers, but all he can see is the enemy. Then Elisha prays God will open his eyes, and in an instant, the hillside around Elisha is filled with horses and chariots of fire.

As the Aramean army advances, Elisha prays again, asking God to make the troops blind. It seems like a strange request based on what the servant has just seen. Why not ask God to open their eyes too? Surely the sight of horses and chariots of fire would lead to a quick retreat.

Instead, Elisha, who isn't recognized by the troops, leads the confused army into the city of Samaria. Only then are their eyes opened again, and the Israelite king asks Elisha if he should kill them. "'Of course not!' Elisha replied. 'Do we kill prisoners of war? Give them food and drink and send them home again to their master.' . . . After that, the Aramean raiders stayed away from the land of Israel" (vv. 22–23).

Elisha models several strategies we can use when we find ourselves in anxiety-provoking confrontations too.

First, Elisha keeps a spiritual perspective rather than just a physical one. While we may not actually see the heavenly army surrounding us as he did, we can trust that God is fighting on our behalf.

Elisha also stays focused on the bigger picture and long-term goal. If he'd simply asked God to let the troops see the horses and chariots, it would have gotten quicker results. But Elisha knew the Aramean army attacking Israel was a chronic problem, so he chose a different tactic. When in a confrontation, we can ask ourselves, "What's the real goal here?"

Then Elisha acts with calm and kindness, the opposite of what the troops expect. By doing so, he communicates, "I'm taking charge of this situation, and I'm not a threat to you." When someone provokes our anxiety or attacks us, it can be easy to lash out. Choosing to show kindness and calmness but not let ourselves get taken advantage of can be powerful.

It's unlikely that a rowdy group of Aramean raiders will show up in our front yard. But confrontation is part of life, and one of the situations most likely to trigger our anxiety. Similar to the response of Elisha's servant, our initial reaction is likely to be fear or despair. We can remember there is a reality greater than what we see, rely on the truth that God has already given us spiritual victory, and respond with holy confidence. Anxiety tells us we have to handle everything on our own, but God promises we will never face any battle alone.

....

God, when I face confrontation, give me eyes to see beyond the human reality. Empower me to respond in faith rather than react in fear. Show me how to reflect both your strength and your love. Amen.

What confrontation has God helped you get through? How did he do so?

THIRTEEN

God Has You Here for Such a Time as This

Who knows if perhaps you were made queen for just such a time as this?

Esther 4:14

Esther looks at her face in a mirror, tilting her head from one side to the other, touching a tiny line that has appeared on her forehead. Has it really been over five years since she first came to the palace? She tries to glimpse the young Jewish girl she was before all this, an orphan grieving her parents, taken in by her cousin Mordecai. Back then, she never would have dreamed she would one day be queen.

Esther hears a knock on the door. "Come in," she says, and one of her maids appears, bowing before her. "Queen Esther," the girl says, "Your cousin Mordecai is at the gate of the palace in burlap and ashes."

Burlap and ashes? This is the ritual of those in mourning. "Get Hathach," she says to the girl, who nods and retreats. Esther tells Hathach, one of the king's eunuchs assigned to be her attendant, to find out why Mordecai is in mourning.

The story Hathach returns with shocks her. Haman, a political leader who is jealous of Mordecai, has persuaded the king to order the destruction of all the Jews in the land. *But*, Esther thinks, *he doesn't know I'm a Jew.* Hathach adds, "Mordecai asks that you go to the king on behalf of your people."

Esther knows the penalty for appearing before the king without an invitation—death. For a moment she hopes Mordecai will understand this. Surely he would never ask such a thing of her. But Hathach later returns with a second message from Mordecai that ends with a question: "Who knows if perhaps you were made queen for just such a time as this?" (Esther 4:14).

Esther looks in the mirror again and sees not the young Jewish girl she searched for earlier but the queen she is now. A woman who has learned how to not just survive but influence, not just rely on her beauty but use her brilliant mind, not just accept her fate but quietly shape it through the power of her faith.

Fear screams she's a fool, but Esther decides, "If I must die, I must die" (v. 16). As she walks into the throne room, her heart pounds, her breathing speeds up, and her hands shake. But the worst doesn't happen. Instead, Esther's actions save her people and are still celebrated during the yearly Jewish festival of Purim.

We will all have moments when we're tempted to choose the safe option, to hold back, to hide. But we need to know that sometimes anxiety is an inevitable part of obedience. God will ask us to step out of our comfort zone. We're human, and when we do so, our fight-or-flight response will be triggered. Our hearts may pound, our breathing might speed up, and our hands could shake. This is biology, but it is not destiny.

There's a myth that says a test of what God wants us to do is "having peace about it." We won't experience fear or anxiety when doing what he wants. But Esther, Moses, and even Jesus in the garden of Gethsemane showed signs of human anxiety when they were right in the middle of God's plan for their lives.

Fear doesn't always mean turn back; sometimes it means move forward.

Faith doesn't mean never feeling anxious; it means obeying anyway.

You, too, are here for such a time as this.

....

God, you have placed me in this world for such a time as this. Open my eyes to what you're asking me to do each day. When the human part of me wants to settle for comfort and safety, give me the strength to be like Esther. Amen.

When was a time in your life that you felt anxiety but took a step of faith anyway?

FOURTEEN

God Speaks to You in the Storm

> Then the LORD spoke to Job out of the storm.
>
> Job 38:1 NIV

Job thinks of all he has lost—his children, his possessions, and even his health. What will he do now? He sits for many days with his friends and processes all he's endured, including his questions, confusion, and frustration. His expressions of emotion include sorrow, rage, despair, and a desire for his life to end.

Finally, the Lord speaks "to Job out of the storm" (Job 38:1 NIV). He asks Job a series of questions like, "Where were you when I laid the earth's foundation?" (v. 4 NIV). At the end, Job says, "My ears had heard of you but now my eyes have seen you" (42:5 NIV). What Job needs most aren't answers to his questions but rather an assurance that God is real and he is still in control despite all that has happened.

In the classic movie *Forrest Gump*, Lieutenant Dan is a Job-like character. Although Forrest saves him from death in the Vietnam War, he still loses both of his legs. Rather than being grateful, Lieutenant Dan experiences increasing bitterness. He eventually joins Forrest on his shrimping boat.

One day a horrendous storm mercilessly batters their vessel. Rather than retreating to the shore, Lieutenant Dan climbs the mast and screams into the wind at God. He vents his rage and despair in a spiritual confrontation that is difficult to listen to because it's so visceral and raw.

But the next time we see Lieutenant Dan, he is swimming peacefully in the sea with a smile on his face. Forrest narrates the scene by saying, "You know what I think? I think that day Lieutenant Dan found God."[1]

Both Job and Lieutenant Dan discover a truth many of us never experience: *whatever we're feeling, God can take it.* We tend to tiptoe around God as if he's a weak old man we shouldn't upset. Or we see him as a heavenly avenger just waiting to send yet another lightning bolt our way. But he loves us unconditionally and is strong enough to handle anything we share with him.

A few years ago, my daughter and I had a serious disagreement. We thundered with our voices and rained down difficult emotions. She was hurt, confused, and angry. When we finished working through the issue, she said something that surprised me: "I feel so loved." I realized in that moment, part of parenting is being able to stay present with your children even when what they have to say is hard to hear, even when what they feel is messy. God does the same with us.

If you have only been sharing with God what you think he wants to hear, then perhaps it's your turn to climb the mast, voice your complaints, and give God the opportunity to speak to you in the storm too.

....

God, you are so much bigger, wiser, and more compassionate than I can even comprehend. Give me the courage to bring all I feel to you, trusting you can take it. Amen.

What are you sometimes afraid to share with God? Tell him about it now.

FIFTEEN

God Is Your Good Shepherd

Even when I walk
    through the darkest valley,
I will not be afraid,
    for you are close beside me.
Your rod and your staff
    protect and comfort me.

Psalm 23:4

David strolls the palace grounds and pauses in front of a man surrounded by a small group of sheep. David picks up one of the smallest lambs and strokes its head. It bleats and he laughs, remembering his childhood, when sheep like these were his closest companions. Long before he was the shepherd of God's people as the king of Israel, David cared for livestock as the youngest son in his family.

He knew intimately the ways and heart of being a shepherd.

He also knew the anxiety and dangers of dark valleys, where a predator or unexpected threat could be waiting behind the next rock. To be prepared, David would have carried two essential tools: a rod and staff, both used for the protection of sheep.

The shepherd's rod provides protection from *external* threats. W. Phillip Keller, author of *A Shepherd Looks at Psalm 23*, says, "The shepherd's rod is an instrument of protection both for himself and his sheep when they are in danger. It is used both as a defense and a deterrent against anything that would attack."[1]

David talks of taking care of his sheep when he tells Saul why he's qualified to fight Goliath. He says, "Your servant has been keeping his father's sheep. When a lion or a bear came and carried off a sheep from the flock, I went after it, struck it and rescued the sheep from its mouth" (1 Sam. 17:34–35 NIV). The apostle Peter describes Jesus as our "Chief Shepherd," and soon after he says the enemy of our souls is "like a roaring lion, looking for someone to devour" (1 Pet. 5:8). When we go through dark valleys, times of difficulty or anxiety when we're more vulnerable to attack, we can trust our Good Shepherd always has our back.

The shepherd's staff provides protection from *internal* threats. Sheep are likely to get themselves into trouble, and so are we—especially when we're in a dark valley. It's tempting to make ourselves better in ways that can lead to destructive consequences. Keller explains,

> Being stubborn creatures, sheep often get into the most ridiculous and preposterous dilemmas. I have seen my own sheep, greedy for one more mouthful of green grass, climb down steep cliffs where they slipped and fell into the sea. Only my long shepherd's staff could lift them out of the water back onto solid ground again.[2]

The staff is used not for punishment but to draw the sheep back toward the shepherd. "God's kindness is intended to lead you to repentance" (Rom. 2:4 NIV). When we've strayed, intentionally or not, the heart of the Good Shepherd is to rescue us and restore our relationship with him. We may feel the staff of God pulling our hearts toward him through his word, caring friends, and other gentle but compelling ways.

Like David, we will go through dark valleys in life. No one experiences mountaintops all the time. But we can know that every time we descend into a valley, our Good Shepherd is with us. He will protect us with his rod, pursue us with his staff, and guide us to the other side.

....

God, you are my Good Shepherd, and I'm so grateful to be in your care. When I go through dark valleys, comfort me with your rod and staff. I trust you to get me through whatever I face. Amen.

How have you seen God use his rod and staff in your life? How has he protected you and drawn you toward him?

SIXTEEN

God Will Give You the Desires of Your Heart

Take delight in the LORD,
> and he will give you your heart's desires.

Commit everything you do to the LORD.
> Trust him, and he will help you.

Psalm 37:4–5

David thinks back over his life. "Once I was young, and now I am old," he writes (Ps. 37:25). He remembers his victory over Goliath—God choosing him, a shepherd boy, to become a king, his mistakes and victories. His children come to mind, especially Solomon, who will soon be king. How can David convey a lifetime of lessons, pass on his legacy, and help his family keep serving God once he's gone?

Psalm 37 seems to be one answer since it's a Hebrew acrostic poem. Each stanza begins with a successive letter of the Hebrew alphabet, a method used to make written words easier to remember. One question it seems David anticipated the generations after him asking is, "How do I know what God wants me to do?"

I asked that question recently while having coffee with a friend. In a season when I needed to make several decisions, I felt stuck at a crossroads, unsure of how to move forward. I explained to my friend that I'd been taught to think of God's will as a tightrope. There was one clear, very specific answer for everything. "That sounds like a lot of pressure," she said, "and I don't think that's how it works."

I had a nagging sense in my soul that she was right. So I went looking in Scripture for how we're to determine God's will. I discovered very few times when God told people *exactly* what to do, as he did with Moses parting the Red Sea. Most of the time he simply wanted people to have an intimate, lifelong relationship with him.

David writes,

> Take delight in the Lord,
>> and he will give you your heart's desires.
>
> Commit everything you do to the Lord.
>> Trust him, and he will help you. (Ps. 37:4–5)

On the surface, this can sound like "delight in God and he'll do what you want." But the opposite is true. When we delight in God, our hearts are in sync with what *he* wants.

Every morning I pray, "God, align my mind with yours. Align my heart with yours. Align my eyes, ears, mouth, hands, and feet with yours." When I shared this with my friend, she said, "Then you can trust that what you choose to do will align with what God wants." Of course I objected, saying, "But what if it's not?" Then I remembered that Romans 8:28 says, "God causes everything to work together for the good of those who love God and are called according to his purpose for them." God can redirect me and even redeem my mistakes as needed.

I thought the root of my indecisiveness was spiritual, but it was really my anxiety. I thought if I could figure out *exactly* what God wanted me to do, then I couldn't possibly fail. I wouldn't get hurt, experience rejection, or have regrets. So I put off making decisions or moving forward.

Yes, God gives us boundaries through clear commands in his Word (no murdering anyone today), and we're encouraged to get godly advice. But God's will isn't a tightrope; it's an invitation to walk with Someone we love for a lifetime.

I'm adding a new line to my prayer each morning: "God, give me the courage to trust myself today because I trust in you." I want more holy risking and less anxious retreating, more mistakes that help me learn and less missed opportunities, more pushing forward and less being paralyzed by fear. When it's my turn to write "once I was young, now I am old," I want to have stories worth passing on and hard-won wisdom to share. I have a feeling you do too.

. . . .

God, align my mind with yours. Align my heart with yours. Align my eyes, ears, mouth, hands, and feet with yours. Give me the courage to trust myself today because I trust in you. Amen.

What piece of advice would you give someone else based on what God has taught you?

SEVENTEEN

God Wants to Give You Rest

> It is useless for you to work so hard
> from early morning until late at night,
> anxiously working for food to eat;
> for God gives rest to his loved ones.
>
> Psalm 127:2

Solomon asks himself a familiar question: "What should I try next?" As the wisest king to ever rule Israel, he has access to everything. No wish goes unfulfilled. No desire is left unmet. No goal is too lofty or dream out of reach. And yet he's still haunted by an anxious restlessness. Nothing quite satisfies his soul. "Everything is meaningless!" (Eccles. 1:2).

Solomon tries to fill the void by

- looking for the good things in life;
- cheering himself with wine;

- building huge homes;
- planting beautiful vineyards;
- making gardens and parks;
- building reservoirs;
- having many servants;
- owning large herds and flocks;
- collecting silver, gold, and treasure;
- hiring entertainment, like singers; and
- having relationships with many women. (Compiled from verses 1–8.)

Anxiety is a high-energy emotion that pushes us to act. We can get stuck in a cycle, as Solomon did, of thinking that "the next thing" will be what we really need. A bigger house. More accomplishments at work. The perfect relationship. But then what we think we wanted never quite soothes our souls in the way we'd hoped.

We often think of Psalms as a book written by David, but it actually has multiple authors, including Solomon. Psalm 127:2 gives us a glimpse into an aha moment Solomon had about his striving. He writes,

> It is useless for you to work so hard
> from early morning until late at night,

> anxiously working for food to eat;
>> for God gives rest to his loved ones.

The lie of anxiety is that something "out there" will give us the calm we crave. So we push ourselves, keep searching, try harder.

But this one phrase in Psalm 127:2 changes everything: "For God gives rest." This kind of rest isn't about a lack of physical activity. God encourages us to enjoy his good gifts, be productive, and take steps of obedience. Instead, this is about resting from anxiety-based striving that exhausts us and leaves us feeling empty.

Anxiety tells us having inner peace is about *what we can get*. The truth is, inner peace is *something only God can give*. When Solomon says, "Everything is meaningless!" (Ecc. 1:2), he's describing all that's temporary and external, not eternal. What our souls truly need can't be bought or built; it can only be bestowed on us by a good God who invites us into grace.

The next time we feel anxiety urging us to act, let's pause and ask, "What does my soul *really* need right now?" As Solomon finally discovered, God invites us not to react to the restlessness we sometimes feel but to rest in his unfailing love.

....

God, give me the wisdom to know when anxiety is pushing me. Pull me back into your love and grace. You are the source of meaning in my life. You are the one who calms my heart and gives me rest. Amen.

What has anxiety been pushing you to do? What does your soul really need today?

EIGHTEEN

God Soothes Your Soul

> I have calmed and quieted myself,
>> like a weaned child who no longer cries for its
>> mother's milk.
> Yes, like a weaned child is my soul within me.
>
> Psalm 131:2

In the Old Testament, God instructed Jews to make three pilgrimages to Jerusalem each year—in spring for Passover, in summer for Shavuot, and in the fall for Sukkot. David had these travelers in mind when he wrote Psalm 131, and it starts with this dedication: "A song for pilgrims ascending to Jerusalem."

Imagine the scene—men walking on dusty roads, children playing tag as they weave in and out of the crowd, mothers with babies swaddled to their chests. It's this last image David brings to mind with the words, "I have calmed and quieted myself, like a weaned child" (Ps. 131:2). It's a picture of contentment, not want; endearment, not distress; satisfaction, not seeking more.

For those of us who struggle with anxiety, being like a weaned child means we've learned to calm ourselves. Before we can calm and quiet our souls as the psalmist says, sometimes we need practical ways to calm our bodies. It's hard to pray when we're in the middle of an anxiety episode.

In recent years, researchers have discovered ways to decrease anxiety that mimic what soothes us as infants. For example, a weighted blanket offers comforting warmth that helps our nervous systems recalibrate (I have two).

Another technique is called self-havening. To practice it, cross your arms and place each hand just below your shoulder. Slowly run your hands down your arms to just above your elbow. Then lift your hands off your arms and return your hands to their original place beneath your shoulders. Take deep breaths in through your nose and out through your mouth as you do self-havening. Repeat this until you feel your body begin to feel calmer.

This action activates our brains in a way similar to when we soothe a baby by holding or stroking them. Alpha brain waves are created when we're stressed out or experiencing trauma. Delta waves are created when we're relaxed and at peace. Self-havening enables our minds to replace alpha waves with delta ones.

Once our bodies calm down, we can turn to quieting our souls. A weaned child no longer connects with her mother from a place of need. It's not just about what she wants, it's about relationship. For the pilgrims, this meant journeying to Jerusalem not to get something, like a favor from God or a prayer answered, but to experience God's presence in new yet familiar ways. For us, this can mean embracing spiritual practices like gratitude, praise, and reflection that aren't need-based but are simply about being with God.

When we feel anxious, we can ask ourselves the following:

- How can I calm and quiet my body (example: self-havening)?
- How can I calm and quiet my mind (example: repeating comforting Scripture)?
- How can I calm and quiet my soul (example: listing things I'm grateful for)?

You can experiment and find what works best for you. The good news? Like a mother with her baby on a pilgrimage, God will be carrying you and caring for you every step of the way.

....

God, I pause now to calm and quiet my soul before you. Thank you for carrying me every step of my journey. My soul is safe with you. Amen.

What helps you calm and quiet yourself when you feel anxious? Write down at least three ideas.

NINETEEN

God Knows Your Thoughts

Search me, O God, and know my heart;

test me and know my anxious thoughts.

Psalm 139:23

David invites God to search, test, and know the most intimate parts of who he is, including his anxiety. Maybe you're far more spiritual than I am and do the same. When I feel anxious, I often don't want God to know what I'm thinking. It feels too messy and vulnerable. Surely I can find a way to get my craziness under control and *then* pray.

Sometimes it goes deeper, and the problem isn't that I don't want to share what I'm thinking with God; it's that I don't even *know* what I'm thinking. I just feel anxious for what seems like no good reason at all. I rush through my day, stressed out and overwhelmed, reacting and exhausting myself without understanding the cause.

So the first step in sharing our anxious thoughts with God is simply to pause and identify them. The part of our brain where anxiety originates isn't verbal; it doesn't use words. That's why when we see a snake right in front of us, we jump back before even needing to tell ourselves, "There's a snake. It looks poisonous. I need to jump approximately two feet backward right now." We simply act in a self-protective way.

A snake usually isn't involved in our everyday anxiety, so it's safe to pause and put words to what we're feeling. Yesterday I found myself in a swirl of anxiety without any obvious cause. I went to a quiet space in my house and prayed, "God, show me the root of what I'm feeling." After sitting in silence for a few moments, I realized an old lie from my past had come back. I was telling myself that if I didn't do a work-related task perfectly, then I'd be a total failure. Of course that made me anxious! Once I knew the source, I could realign my thinking with the truth: *My worth is not defined by my work. God alone gets to tell me who I truly am.*

Research has shown that writing down our anxious thoughts can also help. One way to do so is by creating a Worry Box. Find a box with a lid and cut a slit in the top. You can decorate it or wrap it in paper if you'd like. When you feel anxious about something, write it down on a piece of paper, then slide it into the Worry Box as a physical expression of giving it over to God. Every few months, open the box and write answered prayers on the back of the slips.

What we write on the slips of paper we put into our Worry Box isn't a surprise to God. Psalm 139 actually starts with this:

> O LORD, you have examined my heart
> and know everything about me. (v. 1)

We're not going to shock, overwhelm, or disappoint him with what we share. Asking him to search us and know our anxious thoughts simply means we no longer have to face our anxiety alone. God will be there with us as our helper, guide, and faithful friend.

....

God, search me and know my heart; test me and know my anxious thoughts. Reveal to me the roots of my worries and help me replace them with truth. Thank you that I never have to be alone in my anxiety. Amen.

Practice writing down your worries and releasing them to God.

TWENTY

God Is Greater Than All Your Fears

The fear of the LORD is the beginning of wisdom,
and knowledge of the Holy One is understanding.

Proverbs 9:10 NIV

Where does wisdom come from? Many would say books, education, even life experiences. But Solomon tells us, "Fear of the LORD is the beginning of wisdom" (Prov. 9:10 NIV). When we hear the word *fear*, it can sound strange to us because we don't often use it in a similar way today.

Author and pastor Chuck Swindoll explains, "The fear of the Lord refers to our viewing Him with the respect He deserves. It means living our lives in light of what we know of Him, holding Him in the highest estimation, and depending on Him with humble trust."[1]

As a king himself, Solomon understood this kind of fear because it's what he wanted from those he ruled. Proverbs 24:21 says, "Fear the LORD and the king." So fear like this is about *authority*. Who will we listen to and obey?

Anxiety is bossy. It tells us, "You can't go after that dream, you'll fail." It declares, "You have to be perfect or no one will love you." It threatens, "You must be on guard all the time or something terrible will happen." To silence it, we need to fear something more than its voice in our minds. Only God is big and powerful enough to fulfill that role.

Some of us have been taught a distorted view of God. We've been told he's not a benevolent king but a vindictive dictator. He rules not through love but through punishment. He's waiting with a lightning bolt in hand so he can show us who's in charge. But the God we serve leads through mercy, not manipulation. He humbled himself and dwelled among us. He laid down his life on our behalf. He is good, wise, and kind. We can trust him.

For those who grew up in a legalistic environment like I did, learning the true meaning of fearing God can take time. We need to be patient with ourselves as we come to understand that while we're to have fear *for* God, we don't need to be terrified *of* him. Because of what Jesus did for us on the cross and through his resurrection, we've been made right with God and brought into his endless grace.

William D. Eisenhower says, "As I walk with the Lord, I discover that God poses an ominous threat to my ego, but not to me. He rescues me from my delusions, so he may reveal the truth that sets me free. . . . *Fear of the Lord is the beginning of wisdom, but love from the Lord is its completion*" (emphasis added).[2]

We are to fear God, yet his "perfect love expels all fear" (1 John 4:18). It's a divine paradox; only by fearing God can we start overcoming our fear of everything else. When we fear God, we see him as an authority more powerful than the lies we battle inside. He is our protector and provider, security and salvation, the soother of our souls and the mighty warrior who fights on our behalf.

The fear of God is the beginning of wisdom. It's also part of being set free from our anxiety.

....

God, I fear you and approach you with awe, respect, humility, and trust. You are bigger than all my worries, more powerful than my anxiety, mightier than anything I will ever face. Amen.

What have you been taught about fearing God? How do you see it differently now?

TWENTY-ONE

God Alone Knows Your Future

You can make many plans,
but the LORD's purpose will prevail.

Proverbs 19:21

As king, Solomon spent much of his time making decisions. Life is even more complex now, and researchers estimate we make about 35,000 decisions a day.[1] Many of those are simple, like what to eat for breakfast or which route to take to work. But others can cause us angst, especially if we struggle with anxiety. We become paralyzed by fear and unable to move forward.

When making decisions, our brains naturally predict outcomes. We run imaginary scenarios through our minds. For example, "If I (choose this option), then (this will happen)." This ability to forecast the future can be helpful, but it's also often wildly inaccurate. Why? Our brains naturally picture the worst-case scenario, even if it's highly unlikely to happen.

An exercise that can help with this is creating a chart with three columns. Title the first column "Worst Outcome," the middle "Best Outcome," and the far right one "Most Likely Outcome."

For example, imagine you're trying to decide if you should take a new job. In the Worst Outcome column, you might write, "I am terrible at the new job, get fired, lose my house, and all my friends reject me. I end up broke, homeless, and completely alone." Then in the Best Outcome column, write something like, "I'm the most fabulous employee ever. I'm promoted to CEO in one month, get a raise of a million dollars, and spend my days typing on a laptop from my yacht." Finally, in the Most Likely Outcome column, write a more realistic scenario like, "I show up at the new job, and it feels like the first day of school—a little awkward and nerve-wracking. But I work hard to learn, eventually make some new friends, and it gets easier with time. There are challenges, but I'm growing and glad I made this career change." Next to each outcome, write down the percentage of how likely it is to actually happen on a scale from 0 to 10, where 1 is "not at all likely" and 10 is "absolutely certain."

This exercise not only balances out our tendency to think negatively, but it also reveals an important reality: *we can never be completely sure of what we predict*. We're all just going through life making our best guesses about what will happen. God alone actually knows the future. That's why Proverbs 19:21 is so reassuring:

> You can make many plans,
>> but the LORD's purpose will prevail.

It means that when we seek God, no matter what we choose, he will still accomplish his purpose in our lives.

I have this verse on a canvas print in my office to remind me of this truth. I'm often tempted to believe the lie that unless I get everything exactly right, then everything will go completely wrong. That's a lot of pressure. I'm learning to trust instead that even in my imperfection, in my limitations, in the little that I know, God is able to get me where he wants me to go. He's able to redeem, redirect, and work all things together for my good—and yours too. It's not up to us to get every detail of every decision perfect; our role is simply to depend on him and keep taking one small step after another. *Whew.*

....

God, you alone know my future and where you are leading me. Give me the courage to trust you, to keep moving forward one step at a time, believing your purposes in my life will prevail. Amen.

Try doing the outcome exercise from today's reading.

TWENTY-TWO

God Is in Your Everyday Moments

She is clothed with strength and dignity,
and she laughs without fear of the future.

Proverbs 31:25

onfession: the Proverbs 31 woman used to intimidate me. In just a few verses, she gets up before dawn (you lost me right there), buys a field, makes clothes, runs a business, ensures her family is fed, and laughs at the future while she's doing it all.

Then I discovered the Proverbs 31 woman isn't a description of the original superwoman. Instead, it's an alphabetic acrostic poem illustrating what it means to live with wisdom. This style of writing helped readers more easily memorize the words. The Proverbs 31 woman is about inspiration, not specific instructions. And what inspires me most about this woman is that she doesn't get stuck in her head like I often do. She spins wool instead of worries, gets up early instead of getting worked up, helps the needy instead of telling herself she isn't enough.

What's her secret?

> Charm is deceptive, and beauty does not last;
>   but a woman who fears the LORD will be greatly
>   praised. (Prov. 31:30)

As we've already talked about, the fear of the Lord is the beginning of wisdom and true well-being.

But the Proverbs 31 woman also uses another tactic those of us who struggle with anxiety can apply: she stays connected to the real world—what she can see, hear, touch, smell, and taste. Sometimes we dismiss these things as unspiritual, but they can actually be an essential part of managing our anxiety and being proactive.

Research has shown an effective way to calm ourselves and get out of our heads is the 5 Senses Technique.

First, notice 5 things you can see. Look around you and become aware of your environment. Try to pick out things you don't usually notice.

Second, notice 4 things you can touch. Bring attention to the things you're currently feeling, such as the texture of your clothing or the smooth surface of the table you're resting your hands on.

Third, notice 3 things you can hear. Listen for things in the background you don't normally notice. It could be the birds chirping outside or an appliance humming in the next room.

Fourth, notice 2 things you can smell. Bring attention to scents you usually filter out, either pleasant or unpleasant. Catch a whiff of the pine trees outside or food cooking in the kitchen.

Finally, notice 1 thing you can taste. Take a sip of a drink, chew gum, or note the current taste in your mouth.[1]

We tend to overspiritualize the Proverbs 31 woman, turning her into an ideal we can never attain. We do the same when it comes to dealing with our anxiety. We put pressure on ourselves to find huge and holy solutions. But as the Proverbs 31 woman knew, sometimes it's in the simple, ordinary moments of our lives that we experience God's extraordinary presence when we need it most.

....

God, when I get stuck in my head, reconnect me with the present moment, which is where you always are with me. Help me to see, touch, hear, smell, and taste your goodness all around me. Amen.

Pause and do the exercise from today's reading.

5 Things I Can See

4 Things I Can Touch

3 Things I Can Hear

2 Things I Can Smell

1 Thing I Can Taste

TWENTY-THREE

God Has a Time for Everything in Your Life

For everything there is a season,
 a time for every activity under heaven.

       Ecclesiastes 3:1

God appears to Solomon in a dream and says, "What do you want? Ask, and I will give it to you!" (1 Kings 3:5). Solomon is like a game show contestant picking his prize. What will it be? Riches, fame, power, a new RV? Solomon bypasses all these and simply asks for wisdom. We're all still benefiting from that choice through the words he gave to us in the book of Ecclesiastes.

One insight he shares that's still often quoted is this:

For everything there is a season,
 a time for every activity under heaven. (3:1)

Is that true even of anxiety? Yes, if we smell smoke in our home, it's time to be anxious. If we're swimming in the ocean and see a fin pop up a few feet from us, we need to be concerned. If Godzilla knocks on the window of our office building, we're wise to get worried. Anxiety acts as an alarm system warning us of danger. It's essential to our physical survival and overall well-being.

It's time for anxiety when

1. there's a specific threat (fire, shark, Godzilla) and
2. we need to take swift action (get the fire extinguisher, swim to shore, call security).

Thankfully, dangerous circumstances like these are rare. But our anxiety alarm system still goes off, often in unhelpful ways. A common example is when we worry about someone we love even though there's no reason to believe they're in harm's way and there's nothing we need to do to protect them. We just start picturing a worst-case scenario—a crash, a diagnosis, Godzilla—and find ourselves trapped in a tornado of worry. When our anxiety alarm system goes off, we can pause and ask ourselves two questions: "Is there a specific threat right now?" and "Do I need to take action right away?" If the answer is no, then it's likely unhelpful anxiety.

Ironically, one proven technique to help control unwanted worry is to schedule it. First, choose a daily or weekly time to worry. Find a quiet place to sit, and bring a blank sheet of paper with you. Start a timer for ten minutes. At the top of the paper, write, "God, I'm worried about . . . ," then begin writing down all your worries. Give yourself permission to feel whatever emotions come up. When the timer goes off, take a few deep breaths and write at the bottom of the page, "God, I give all these worries to you."

When anxiety arises between your scheduled worry sessions, tell yourself, "I will worry about that when it's time." Then shift your mind to something else. Repeat this as much as you need to throughout your day. Making this a habit will help you control your anxiety rather than it control you. (Note: If you find it impossible to stop worrying and it's interfering with your daily life, work, or relationships, then you might have an anxiety disorder. Contact a trusted professional, like a counselor, who can identify what's going on and create a treatment plan with you.)

It's easy to tell ourselves we should *never* be anxious. But that's not realistic or even healthy. As wise Solomon knew, there really is a time for everything—even anxiety.

....

God, give me the wisdom to know when anxiety is helpful and when it's not. Give me the courage and self-discipline to bring all that concerns me to you. Amen.

Try the technique shared in today's reading by setting a timer now for ten minutes and writing down your worries. If you don't have time to do so now, schedule it for when you do.

TWENTY-FOUR

God Is Bigger Than Any News Headline

Don't be afraid, for I am with you.

  Don't be discouraged, for I am your God.

I will strengthen you and help you.

  I will hold you up with my victorious right hand.

Isaiah 41:10

Isaiah the prophet walks the streets of Jerusalem, praying and overhearing bits of conversation.

"Did you hear what happened?"

"The world keeps getting worse."

"Our leaders need to do something."

Talk about politics and social problems permeates every area of life, from the public synagogue to private dinner tables. All that talking has left little room for the voice of God, and the Jewish people are experiencing the consequences. The northern kingdom of Israel has been taken into captivity by a pagan nation. The southern kingdom of Judah, where Isaiah lives, faces the danger of the same fate.

God calls Isaiah to speak his heart to his wayward people, whose choices are leading to devastating consequences. God doesn't sugarcoat their rebellion and the destruction it will bring. But he also never stops loving them and calling them back to him. It's in this context that one of the most often quoted verses in Scripture appears.

> Don't be afraid, for I am with you.
>> Don't be discouraged, for I am your God.
> I will strengthen you and help you.
>> I will hold you up with my victorious right hand.
>> (Isa. 41:10)

This verse was first written for a specific nation at a particular time in history, but it still speaks to us as God's people today. We live in a time very similar to that of Isaiah—one where politics, division, and social injustice abound. It's easy to think a leader, political party, or new law is the solution. But Isaiah reminds us of the one sure thing in our lives . . . *God himself.*

Don't be afraid, for I am with you. God's presence is pervasive and permanent. He is with us in every moment, each situation, and whatever circumstances we face. He has promised to never leave or forsake us.

Don't be discouraged, for I am your God. Human leaders will fail us. Politicians will make promises they won't keep. God is the only authority who is completely trustworthy, who will never disillusion us or let us down.

I will strengthen you and help you. We don't have to rely on our own power or handle everything by ourselves. God will give us what we need to persevere and keep pursuing his will, one day at a time.

I will hold you up with my victorious right hand. God's right hand symbolizes his strength, authority, and blessing. When we're weary of all that's going on in the world, God will support and sustain us. The battle is his, and with him we can't be defeated.

Isaiah is also the book of the Bible with the most prophecies about the Messiah. In the middle of all that was happening, God's people could have hope because Jesus was coming. There will always be scary news headlines, wars, diseases, and everyday difficulties. In the middle of all that's *still* happening, we can have hope because Jesus is coming again.

Isaiah reminded God's people of what was true, and it's what we need to hear today too.

God is not done with history.

He's not done with your story either.

....

God, sometimes all that's going on in our world feels scary and overwhelming. You are my hope, and I choose to trust in you no matter what happens. When I'm tempted to let news headlines determine my day, help me remember that you alone get the final say. Amen.

Which of the four phrases in Isaiah 41:10 (refer back to the reading if needed) did you most need to hear today? Why?

TWENTY-FIVE

God Will Get You Through

> When you go through deep waters,
>   I will be with you.
> When you go through rivers of difficulty,
>   you will not drown.
> When you walk through the fire of oppression,
>   you will not be burned up;
>   the flames will not consume you.
>
> Isaiah 43:2

When you go through deep waters . . .
   Noah and the ark, safe in the flood until dry land appeared again.

When you go through rivers of difficulty . . .
   The people of Israel finally crossing the Jordan into the promised land after the wilderness.

When you walk through the fire of oppression . . .

Shadrach, Meshach, and Abednego thrown into the furnace and emerging untouched by the flames.

When the prophet Isaiah spoke those words, stories like these would have come to mind for God's people. And God is still writing stories of his faithfulness— showing up in our everyday lives, in the middle of our anxiety, reminding us that he is with and for us.

My husband, Mark, and I are in a challenging season of our lives. We went for a walk yesterday to clear our minds and catch our breath. When we started out, the skies looked clear. But about halfway through, drops of rain began to fall, softly at first, then with force. Far from home, we had no choice but to keep walking.

As we did so, I thought of how the situation we were in felt like walking through the rain. Isaiah 43:2 came to mind, and I remembered one word appears in it three times—*through*. When hard times come or anxiety strikes, I often want a different word—*out*. I gladly would have let a helicopter pick me up and transport me and Mark out of the rain yesterday. I wish I had a magic eject button that would instantly get the two of us out of our current circumstances too.

But that's not real life. There's usually no easy way out, only more persevering. Mark and I had many more steps to take before we could get to somewhere dry. What I sensed in those rainy moments was God whispering that he would be with us, this challenge wouldn't overcome us, and we'd be okay no matter what happened. Whatever you're facing, he's whispering that to your heart today too.

Getting through doesn't mean getting what you want. It means having what you need in each moment regardless of the results. The cancer might not instantly disappear, but at every doctor's appointment, during each round of chemo, in the waiting rooms, in times of wondering, he will get you through.

The prodigal might not return tomorrow, but every time you pray, when the phone rings with news you don't want, in the nights when you worry about the future, he will get you through.

The challenges at work might not resolve in one meeting, but in every tense conversation, with each difficult project, in all the seemingly impossible tasks, he will go through it with you.

We are not alone in our deep waters.

We are not forsaken in our rivers of difficulty.

We are not abandoned to the flames.

No, we are God's people, and we are pressing on, refusing to give up, remembering we are loved in every circumstance. He will get us through.

....

God, you are the one with me in every difficult moment. I trust you will get me through whatever I face. You have never forsaken me, and you never will. Give me the strength I need today to persevere, and remind me you are here. Amen.

What are you facing right now? How is God helping you get through it?

TWENTY-SIX

God Is Calling You

> Don't be afraid of the people, for I will be with you and will protect you. I, the LORD, have spoken!
>
> Jeremiah 1:8

Who would you choose for a prophet? Someone from a small town or a sophisticated city, an amateur or an experienced pro, a charismatic speaker or a reluctant communicator? God picks Jeremiah, an inexperienced small-town priest who scholars believe was only about twenty years old. God calls Jeremiah with these words:

> I knew you before I formed you in your mother's womb.
>   Before you were born I set you apart
>   and appointed you as my prophet to the nations.
>   (Jer. 1:4–5)

Rather than replying with enthusiasm, Jeremiah protests, "O Sovereign LORD . . . I can't speak for you! I'm too young!" (v. 6). Has anxiety ever caused you to respond in a similar way to something God is asking you to do? We're all tempted to believe we're "too" something.

Too young.

Too old.

Too quiet.

Too loud.

Too much.

Too little.

God addresses the real cause for Jeremiah's pause: "Don't be afraid of the people" (v. 8). When we say we're "too" something, usually we're worried about what people will think of us. Considering how others will view us is a natural and healthy part of being human. Daniel Goleman, a bestselling author and science journalist, says, "We are wired to connect. Neuroscience has discovered our brain's design makes it sociable."[1] God created us to consider what people think of us; he just doesn't want us to be controlled by it. What he said to Jeremiah is true for us too: "I will be with you and will protect you" (1:8).

When I was about the same age as Jeremiah, a counselor diagnosed me with social anxiety. This condition is an intense and persistent fear of being judged by others that interferes with everyday life. Like Jeremiah, I felt called by God to write and speak publicly, but even calling a restaurant to order a pizza scared me silly. How could God use me?

Over two decades later, I still struggle with my social anxiety sometimes. But I've learned to *feel the fear and do it anyway*. Standing backstage before speaking to a crowd of eight thousand people, I thought about how far God had brought me. Working with my counselor helped, and I'd recommend anyone struggling with significant anxiety to find a trusted counselor too. I also had an aha moment that helped me see my fear differently. I realized, *we are afraid when something matters to us*. The only way to completely stop being afraid is to stop caring.

Jeremiah cared about the messages God entrusted to him and the people he served as a prophet for the next forty years. The phrase "do not be afraid" appears several more times in his writing. Through Jeremiah, we see that "do not be afraid" isn't a condemning command; it's a soul-comforting challenge to move past our fear and into obedience because God is always with and for us.

Jeremiah felt the fear and obeyed anyway.

Let's choose to do the same today.

....

God, I never want fear to get in the way of what you're calling me to do. Give me the courage to listen to your voice, believe you can use me, and trust your plan for my future. Amen.

How does anxiety tell you to finish this sentence: "I'm too . . ."? What truth does God want to tell you instead today?

TWENTY-SEVEN

God Is Your Ultimate Certainty

The faithful love of the LORD never ends!
His mercies never cease.
Great is his faithfulness;
his mercies begin afresh each morning.

Lamentations 3:22–23

Jerusalem, once so full of people, is now deserted"
(Lam. 1:1). Reading these words, it's easy to picture the prophet Jeremiah (believed to be the author of Lamentations) walking through empty streets. Gone are the signs of life and joy, the sound of singing, the laughter of children, the friendly bargaining in the market. Babylon has invaded and destroyed the once glorious city.

Yet in the middle of mourning, Jeremiah offers words of hope that we still often quote today:

> The faithful love of the LORD never ends!
>   His mercies never cease.
> Great is his faithfulness;
>   his mercies begin afresh each morning.
>   (Lam. 3:22–23)

When anxiety enters our lives, it can feel like an invasion. Our peace is stolen, our happiness ransacked, our energy depleted. But the same truth remains: God is faithful; his love and mercy never end.

When we're dealing with difficult circumstances or anxiety, we need security. When everything is changing, we need to know what will always be the same. In those moments, God himself says he will be our certainty. Even when the whole world falls apart, even when all we can feel is the frantic racing of our hearts, he is our steady, ever-present strength.

To show us this is true, God has provided things we can count on in the world around us. Each sunrise reminds us his mercies are new every morning. Every sunset tells us that even as night comes, he is still in control. These rhythms in nature soothe us. Imagine if every day the sun rose and set at a different time, if nothing in nature was orderly or predictable. We'd experience confusion and chaos.

We can align with this part of God's character and design by creating "certainty anchors" in our daily lives as well. Author Jonathan Fields explains it this way:

> A certainty anchor is a practice or process that adds something known and reliable to your life when you may otherwise feel you're spinning off in a million different directions. Rituals and routines can function as certainty anchors; their power comes from the simple fact that they are always there. They are grounding experiences to which you can always return, no matter what's going on. Their consistency makes them effective tools to counter the anxiety that comes . . . from living in uncertain times.[1]

If you're in an anxiety-provoking season of life, rhythms and routines are even more important than when life is calm and predictable. The key is to keep them simple and doable. For example, reading this book each morning is a certainty anchor. Going for an afternoon walk, journaling before bed at night, talking to a loved one each day, or taking a few minutes to pray can all be certainty anchors too. Notice what soothes and strengthens you, then repeat it. This isn't about doing something complicated; it's about consistency.

In a changing world, we can count on a God of sunrises and sunsets, of faithful love, of mercies that are new every morning because that's how often we need them.

. . . .

God, it's reassuring to know your faithful love never ends and your mercies are new every morning. Help me create rhythms in my life that reflect your consistency and care. Amen.

What's one certainty anchor you already have in your life or you can add today?

TWENTY-EIGHT

God Hears All Your Prayers

Daniel answered, "Long live the king! My God sent his angel to shut the lions' mouths so that they would not hurt me."

Daniel 6:21–22

We talked about certainty anchors yesterday, and Daniel is one of the most powerful examples of using prayer in this way.

Daniel opens the window of his upstairs room facing Jerusalem. Memories from long ago flash through his mind. The Babylon army entering his city. The point of a soldier's sword in his back and the order, "Keep walking." Daniel and his people traveling dusty roads, captives in a pagan land.

Daniel was chosen to enter the royal service and given a new name, Belteshazzar, which meant "Baal's prince." Baal, the foreign god whose prophets Elijah had defeated. Baal, the one the Israelites were forbidden to serve. *Never*, thought Daniel. *I will never bow to any god but the true one of Israel.*

Years later, because of God's favor, the king plans to give Daniel control of the entire empire. Jealous officials convince the king to issue a decree they know Daniel will not obey: pray only to the king or be thrown into a den of lions.

So be it, thinks Daniel as he takes a deep breath, kneels, and gives thanks to God, as he does three times every day. The knock on the door doesn't surprise him. Nor do the sneers on the faces of the officials as they say, "You know the rules."

The king comes to the lions' den early the next morning. "Daniel, servant of the living God! Was your God, whom you serve so faithfully, able to rescue you from the lions?" Daniel answers, "Long live the king! My God sent his angel to shut the lions' mouths so that they would not hurt me" (Dan. 6:20–22).

Daniel surely felt some physical anxiety, a pounding heart, or the speeding up of his breath as he was thrown into the lions' den. But throughout all that happened— being taken captive, receiving threats from rivals, even facing death, he seemed to have had a supernatural steadiness.

What was his secret? Part of it appeared to be his rhythm of praying three times a day. Whatever was going on his world, regardless of what he might have been facing in his royal role, even when he experienced intense opposition, Daniel paused to pray. Like an elite athlete practicing, he trained himself to respond to anxiety-provoking situations with three steps: *pause, pray, repeat.*

Researchers have found that meditation (and re-peated prayer is one form) causes changes in our brains. In particular, long-term meditators have thicker prefrontal cortexes, the area of the brain responsible for higher-order brain function, like awareness, concen-tration, and decision-making. Researchers discovered a corresponding decrease in lower-order functions of the brain, like fear and anxiety. Prayer is a form of meditation that trains our brains to override our anxiety response.

The key to this kind of transformation is consistency. It's natural (and also beneficial) to throw up a prayer when we begin to feel anxious. But for our brains to actually change, it takes practice and persistence. We need to know how to master our anxiety before the lions' den, not when we get thrown in.

Daniel chose a rhythm that fit his life—kneel and pray three times a day. What's a similar rhythm that would work for you? There's no right or wrong way to pray, just choose what is simple and sustainable for you in this season. You might start the day with a prayer of gratitude, meditate on Scripture for a few moments while you get ready in the morning, or intentionally pray at meals or before you go to sleep at night.

Daniel's life shows us that little things done consistently can make a big difference when it matters most.

· ·

God, I'm grateful you invite me to connect with you anytime, anywhere, for any reason. Show me how to do so not just spontaneously but also consistently and intentionally. Help me train my heart, mind, and soul so that I'm ready for whatever comes. Amen.

What rhythm, like praying three times a day, would you like to try this week? If it works for you, keep doing it. If it doesn't, try something else until you discover what's sustainable long term.

TWENTY-NINE

God Will Bring New Life and Growth

Surely the LORD has done great things!
    Don't be afraid, O land.
Be glad now and rejoice,
    for the LORD has done great things.
Don't be afraid, you animals of the field,
    for the wilderness pastures will soon be green.
The trees will again be filled with fruit;
    fig trees and grapevines will be loaded down once more.

Joel 2:20–22

The prophet Joel looks out over desolate land, where sheep struggle to find grass and the branches are bare. He writes words that portray a different time, one of life and growth. The wilderness will be green again. The trees will bear fruit. This is not the end.

God's people experienced a season of loss and destruction because of their rebellion. But even when we are obedient, we'll still experience difficult times. Scripture has a recurring theme of barrenness followed by blessing, death followed by resurrection, loss followed by restoration. What can help us in those in-between times when life feels like it's on hold?

I'm writing this more than a year into the COVID-19 pandemic. I don't know why this happened to humanity. What I do know is that this season has taken a toll on all of us. Author Adam Grant wrote an article in which he describes the emotional state many of us are experiencing as "languishing."[1] It's "the absence of well-being" accompanied by "a sense of stagnation and emptiness."[2]

Hopefully, by the time you're reading this, the pandemic will be only a memory. But we still need to understand languishing, because it can happen at other times as well. When we encounter a crisis, our fight-or-flight response kicks in and we experience anxiety. While uncomfortable, anxiety is also energizing. But if the crisis drags on, like a long pandemic, an extended period of caregiving, or an unresolved loss like infertility, we eventually exhaust our emergency fight-or-flight system. In place of anxiety, we may experience a profound sense of apathy and exhaustion—languishing.

What can we do when this happens? First, we can trust God is still working while we're waiting. Trust is not an emotion, it's a decision we make all over again each day. If you still struggle with challenging feelings, that's okay.

It's also important to allow ourselves to grieve what we've lost. Sometimes losses are tangible, like a job or a person we love. But they can also be invisible, like a dream, our sense of safety, or our old "normal." When we process loss rather than deny it, we don't dismiss what's coming or doubt what God is doing—we make room for it.

We can also adjust our expectations of ourselves and others. In seasons of languishing, we're not going to have the same level of productivity. It's okay to celebrate tiny steps and little wins. Did you get out of bed today? Hooray! Take a shower? Way to go! Manage to mark one thing off your to-do list? Well done!

We can also look for even the smallest signs of new life and growth. Maybe you laugh hard for the first time in a while, find the energy to text a friend, or sense a spark of creativity returning again. Spring is arriving here, and the trees have buds on them. They're not yet fully in bloom, but looking at their branches reminds me that change is coming soon.

If we don't understand languishing, we can lose hope because it seems we'll feel this way forever. But Solomon wisely writes,

For everything there is a season,
a time for every activity under heaven. (Eccles. 3:1)

My grandmother Eula, who is almost ninety, has another way of expressing a similar sentiment: "This too shall pass." She also likes to say, "The Lord is faithful." In the best or worst of times, in celebration and sorrow, in laughter and languishing, in every season of change, who God is remains the same.

. . . .

God, it's a relief to know that even in the seasons when I feel weary, you are still working. When I'm languishing, you bring new life and growth to my soul. Amen.

What's a difficult season you've gone through? How did God help you?

THIRTY

God Gives You Truth for Temptation

> Then Jesus was led by the Spirit into the wilderness to be tempted there by the devil.
>
> Matthew 4:1

Before the start of his public ministry, Jesus faces a private showdown with the enemy. After fasting in the wilderness for forty days, the devil appears and tries to lead him astray.

Most of us are familiar with this story, but how can it help with our anxiety? The temptation of Jesus is ultimately a battle between lies and truth. Those of us who struggle with anxiety need to know how to handle this kind of combat as well. Not all anxiety comes from lies, but we're more vulnerable to believing them when we're anxious.

First, the enemy says, "If you are the Son of God, tell these stones to become loaves of bread" (Matt. 4:3).

Lie: *You have to prove who you are by what you can do*. We can tell we believe this lie when we hustle for approval, define our worth by our success, and refuse to do anything that might include a risk of failure. Jesus responds, "No! The Scriptures say, 'People do not live by bread alone, but by every word that comes from the mouth of God'" (v. 4). Truth: *God will take care of me, and he alone gets the final say in my life.*

So the devil goes a different direction and takes Jesus to the highest point of the temple and tells him to jump off because God will protect him. Lie: *You are completely in control of your personal safety*. We can tell we believe this lie when we get hyperfocused on nothing bad ever happening to us or those we love. But Jesus sees the bigger picture. "You must not test the Lord your God" (v. 7). Truth: *I'm not in complete control of my personal safety (or the safety of those I love), but God does promise me true security no matter what happens.*

The devil tries one more time by taking Jesus to the peak of a high mountain, showing him the kingdoms of the world and their glory, and promising to give Jesus all this if he will do one thing—worship him. Lie: *Satisfaction in life comes from what we can see and obtain*. We can tell if we believe this lie when we wear ourselves out chasing what's "bigger and better." Jesus says, "You must worship the Lord your God and serve only him" (v. 10).

Truth: *Satisfaction comes from aligning with our true purpose, serving, and worshiping the God who created us.*

Think of what causes you the most anxiety. Then ask, "What is the lie behind this?" A lie I often struggle with is, "I don't have what it takes." But the truth is, "By his divine power, God has given us everything we need for living a godly life" (2 Pet. 1:3).

Sometimes we can have the unrealistic expectation that as soon as we speak the truth, our anxiety will disappear. But Jesus had multiple rounds of combating lies before he won his battle in the wilderness. We're not spiritual failures if our anxiety doesn't go away after we quote one verse of Scripture. What matters is continuing to fight lies with truth until we experience victory. This might take minutes, days, weeks, or sometimes years.

We also may need backup. After his temptation, "angels came and took care of Jesus" (v. 11). It's not likely we'll have actual angels show up, but we can look for humans who remind us of them. That might be a trusted counselor, supportive friend, or even an author in a book who helps us keep believing what's true.

We can take comfort in knowing that even Jesus, the Son of God, was tempted to believe lies. He understands what it's like, and he will empower us to live in the truth.

....

God, you are the one who helps me have victory. Show me the lies I've believed and set me free with your truth. Amen.

What's a lie your anxiety tempts you to believe? What's the truth?

THIRTY-ONE

God Is Your Caretaker

That is why I tell you not to worry about everyday life—whether you have enough food and drink, or enough clothes to wear. Isn't life more than food, and your body more than clothing?

Matthew 6:25

A crowd gathers to hear Jesus speak, much like a modern congregation having an outdoor service. The intent in both places is to pay attention, but we all know that's hard to do. One study showed the human mind wanders 47 percent of the time.[1] (So, no, you're not the only one trying to listen to a sermon and thinking about lunch instead.)

The challenging part of this mind-wandering is that the same study also found thoughts "almost always wander to negative thoughts" and get "stuck in rumination."[2] Thinking about lunch reminds us we need to get groceries, which makes us think about how much that will cost, which brings to mind how our boss mentioned possible layoffs in a meeting last week. Suddenly we find ourselves in a vortex of worry and what-ifs that takes us out of the present moment and into an unknown future.

Worry differs from anxiety in that it's specific and usually about something in our external circumstances. Jesus addresses this when he says, "I tell you not to worry about everyday life—whether you have enough food and drink, or enough clothes to wear. Isn't life more than food, and your body more than clothing?" (Matt. 6:25).

As an antidote for worry, Jesus tells the crowd to look at the birds and how God feeds them, at the lilies and how God dresses them (see vv. 26, 28). By doing so, yes, Jesus reminds us of God's care. But he also gives us a practical strategy to combat rumination. When we ruminate, we get "stuck in our heads." To break this cycle, we can take four steps.

Be present. When we worry, we're not in the current moment. As we've talked about, we can use our senses to bring us back to the here and now. Jesus says, "Look at the birds" (v. 26). We can start by taking a deep breath and intentionally observing what's around us.

Practice gratitude. Worry is negative thinking and focuses on what we don't have or might lose. Jesus reminds the crowd of God's care for the birds and lilies as examples of how he cares for each of us too. We can ask

131

ourselves, "What's one way God is taking care of me right now?" Then follow that by expressing our thanks.

Fill the space. Worry is out-of-control thinking, which is one reason it often happens when our minds wander. To stop worrying, we need to fill that space with something else. That can be a phrase we repeat like, "God cares for me." It might also be occupying our mind in another way, like going for a walk or having a conversation with a friend.

Repeat, repeat, repeat. Worry is a natural part of being human—*everyone* worries. We can get frustrated when we do the hard work of getting out of rumination, only to find the same thoughts coming back. When we notice ourselves starting to worry again, we can repeat the first three steps.

It's spring here, and I just opened my window. A robin is building a nest in a tree. Wildflowers are blooming around the little pond behind our house. They don't seem worried or hurried, stressed-out or weary. God is taking good care of them today, and he promises to do the same for us too.

. . . .

God, thank you for taking care of the birds, the flowers, and me. When my mind tries to wander into worry, bring it back to the present—the place where you are with me right now, providing my every need. Amen.

Writing down our worries can help us gain control over them. What's a specific worry you have right now? Go through the process in today's reading to help your mind move past it. (Remember, you may need to do this more than once throughout the day, and that's okay.)

THIRTY-TWO

God Is Your Guru

Then Jesus said, "Come to me, all of you who are weary and carry heavy burdens, and I will give you rest. Take my yoke upon you. Let me teach you, because I am humble and gentle at heart, and you will find rest for your souls. For my yoke is easy to bear, and the burden I give you is light."

Matthew 11:28–30

Be a guru," a marketing consultant once told me. "Everyone wants someone to tell them what to do." The advice struck me as strange until I scrolled through social media with this in mind. I saw every kind of expert—food, fitness, fashion, family, faith. Each one had discovered *the* way to success.

The desire for gurus isn't new. The Pharisees and Sadducees were the self-appointed experts of their time. They claimed to know how to get people on God's good side and created 613 rigid rules that added pressure in almost every area of life.

While it sounds like this would never happen in our modern world, as I read the posts of the many experts in my social media feed, I find myself becoming increasingly anxious. I need to not only eat healthy, but I should eat only organic, straight-from-the-farm salad. I should not only move my body, but I need to do four hundred sit-ups a day. Not only do I need to pray, but I should set a timer and follow a particular formula if I really want God's favor.

When someone shares anything that makes us feel heavy, as if we're being handed a burden, we need to beware. Jesus says about the Pharisees, "They crush people with unbearable religious demands and never lift a finger to ease the burden" (Matt. 23:4).

Are the gurus on my social media Pharisees? No, and I believe many of them are truly trying to help people. But when I take their advice as a *must*, then I'm making them Pharisees in my own mind. Suddenly I'm filled with anxiety because I'm not living up to the standards of someone who likely doesn't even know I exist.

Here are some questions we should ask ourselves:

- When I listen to this person, does my heart feel heavier or lighter?
- Are the words *should* or *have to* used?
- Do I experience guilt and shame when I try to live this way?

- Are those who fail labeled (loser, failure, weak), or is there encouragement and support?

In contrast to the Pharisees, Jesus says, "I am humble and gentle at heart, and you will find rest for your souls. For my yoke is easy to bear, and the burden I give you is light" (Matt. 11:29–30). Gurus tell us, "Here's the way you have to do it." Jesus says, "I am the Way." Instead of striving, he invites us to rest. Instead of being perfect, he offers us freedom and forgiveness. Instead of making life about performance, he brings us into perfect love.

Learning from others can be helpful, and we live in a time with an extraordinary amount of information. That is a gift, but we also need to be aware of when it starts being a source of anxiety and guilt.

We don't need more gurus; we need more grace.

....

God, thank you for being the ultimate source of truth and grace. When I place "shoulds" on my shoulders, help me choose the lightness and freedom you offer instead. Amen.

What's a "should" you've taken on because someone else said you had to? What does God say instead?

THIRTY-THREE

God Is Your Supplier and Multiplier

Then he took the seven loaves and the fish, thanked God for them, and broke them into pieces. He gave them to the disciples, who distributed the food to the crowd.

Matthew 15:36

The disciples stand on a hill near the Sea of Galilee and look out at the crowd with both weariness and wonder. A young man tosses his crutches aside and does a little dance as his friends cheer. A child points out a bird to his mother as he sees one for the first time. A woman who couldn't speak when she arrived throws her head back and laughs.

Jesus, who has been healing people in the crowd for three days, calls the disciples over and says, "I feel sorry for these people. . . . They have nothing left to eat. I don't want to send them away hungry, or they will faint along the way" (Matt. 15:32).

After witnessing miracle after miracle, the disciples respond with what sounds like doubt: "Where would we get enough food here in the wilderness for such a huge crowd?" (v. 33). Jesus has not only repeatedly done the impossible in front of them, but he also fed a huge crowd with only a few loaves and fish just one chapter ago in Matthew 14. So what's going on with the disciples?

I'd like to tell you I can't relate to their response at all. But when I feel exhausted and someone asks yet one more thing of me, it triggers my anxiety. All rational thought and/or faith temporarily goes out the window. I just feel panic that *it's all too much and I'm not enough*. I don't pause to reflect on all the times God has come through for me or how I don't have to rely on my strength. I don't realize that if he's inviting me to do something, then he'll give me what I need.

Thankfully, Jesus doesn't rebuke the disciples. Instead, he asks a simple question: "How much bread do you have?" (v. 34). "Then he took the seven loaves and the fish, thanked God for them, and broke them into pieces. He gave them to the disciples, who distributed the food to the crowd" (v. 36).

In the moments when we feel "not enough," this story offers us hope and help. First, it reassures us that we can offer God what we have, even if it feels like very little. In his hands, there is no such thing as "small."

Then we can follow Jesus's example by saying, "God, thank you." Why? Gratitude is an attitude of abundance, not scarcity. It shifts our perspective from what we lack to what God provides.

Jesus then breaks the loaves and fish. I don't believe he breaks us, but I know from personal experience he can use us when we're broken. Our hurts and imperfections often turn out to be our greatest ministry.

Finally, Jesus gives the food to the disciples so they can share it with others. We don't have to be the ultimate source of what others need; we're only to pass on what we've already received.

Anxiety tells us we're inadequate, God says nothing is impossible with him.

Anxiety whispers we don't have what it takes, God reminds us all we really need is to trust him.

Anxiety says we're going to fall short or mess up, God promises to be not only our supplier but also our multiplier.

. . . .

God, anxiety tries to tell me I'm limited by my human capabilities. But you tell me that with you, nothing is impossible for me. You are my strength when I'm weak. You are my supplier when the needs seem like too much. You are the Savior who still empowers me to serve others. Amen.

Think of the last time you felt the panic the disciples did, a moment when you felt inadequate. Looking back, how can you see God providing for and through you?

THIRTY-FOUR

God Lets You Draw Near

Then the frightened woman, trembling at the realization of what had happened to her, came and fell to her knees in front of him and told him what she had done. And he said to her, "Daughter, your faith has made you well. Go in peace. Your suffering is over."

Mark 5:33–34

The woman draws her cloak around her face, trying to hide her identity. *You shouldn't be here. You shouldn't do this. It's too late for you.* Twelve years ago, she started bleeding and never stopped. She thinks of the humiliating visits to doctors, the last of her money being spent with no relief, the agony of her isolation.

She sees a Pharisee in the crowd, one she's gone to for help. He quotes a verse to her before turning and walking away: "If a woman has a flow of blood for many days that is unrelated to her menstrual period, or if the blood continues beyond the normal period, she is ceremonially unclean. As during her menstrual period, the woman will be unclean as long as the discharge continues" (Lev. 15:25).

Could she dare approach another holy man, this Jesus she's heard so much about? Will he have compassion on her or will he condemn her, throw her out?

Anxiety tells her to turn back, give up, accept her fate. But a flicker of hope burns inside her. She won't bother Jesus. She won't talk to him or share her story. He won't even know she's there. The crowd surges forward, and she finds herself next to him. She reaches out her hand and touches the edge of his robe.

She feels the power flow through her, the warmth of love and belonging, healing and wholeness, restoration and all things being made right. Then Jesus turns and asks, "Who touched my robe?" (Mark 5:30). She knows the possible consequences of revealing herself. "An unclean person in general had to avoid that which was holy and take steps to return to a state of cleanness. Uncleanness placed a person in a 'dangerous' condition under threat of divine retribution, even death, if the person approached the sanctuary."[1]

She has approached God in the flesh, touched him when she is unclean. "Trembling at the realization of what . . . happened to her," she falls "to her knees in front of him" and tells him what she's done (v. 33). Then she waits for the rebuke, the harsh words, her punishment. Instead, Jesus says, "Daughter, your faith has made you well. Go in peace. Your suffering is over" (v. 34). *Daughter*—a term of endearment, acceptance, welcome, love, affection. She'd hoped for physical healing, but this is more than she'd imagined. Her heart, mind, and soul feel whole again too.

Our anxiety can make us feel like this woman. It can go on for years. We may visit many doctors, try many cures. Religious people might rebuke us, make us feel "less than" in our faith. Perhaps we even worry God is mad at us. Can we touch the edge of Jesus's robe too?

My story is not one of instant healing from anxiety. It's likely yours isn't either. Why? I don't know, and I probably won't until heaven. But what speaks deeply to me in this story is that we have a God who is approachable. We're invited to do *more* than just touch the edge of his robe. We have full access to his presence and power whenever we need it.

Anxiety will lie to us and say God wants us only once we're whole. But the truth is, we can come to him anytime we need to, in whatever condition we're in, knowing his response will always be one of love, grace, and understanding.

We are not strangers in a crowd to God. We are his beloved daughters and sons.

....

God, thank you for seeing the suffering anxiety causes in my life and responding not with a rebuke but with great care and affection. I'm reaching out to you today. Amen.

What do you need from Jesus today? Take a moment to tell him.

THIRTY-FIVE

God Will Calm Your Heart

When Jesus woke up, he rebuked the wind and the raging waves. Suddenly the storm stopped and all was calm.

Luke 8:24

Jesus says to his disciples, "Let's cross to the other side of the lake" (Luke 8:22). It's not the first time they've made this short journey. The Sea of Galilee is small, only thirteen miles from north to south and seven miles from east to west. Jesus settles in for a nap, weary from ministering to so many people.

The Sea of Galilee is known for its violent storms. One minute can bring blue skies, the next fierce winds and rain. The lake is surrounded by hills with steep sides, and cold air rushing over the edges collides with warmer air around the water, causing waves up to ten feet high.

I grew up close to the ocean, and I remember going to the beach with my parents. They taught me the water was to be enjoyed but also respected. The ocean was wild—both beautiful and destructive, life-giving and deadly, a playmate and a potential enemy. The disciples, especially Peter and Andrew as fishermen, likely had a similar attitude toward the Sea of Galilee.

We're going to die, the disciples think as panic floods their minds and water begins to fill the boat. Where is Jesus? Why isn't he doing anything? They find him still sleeping and wake him with a fear-filled question: "Teacher, don't you care that we're going to drown?" (Mark 4:38).

What Jesus speaks to the wind and waves seems fitting for the hearts of the disciples too: "Silence! Be still!" (v. 39). The storm suddenly stops, and there is great calm. With terror and amazement, the disciples ask each other, "Who is this man?" (Luke 8:25).

This miracle happens fairly early in Jesus's ministry, and this question reveals that his disciples are still trying to figure him out. They've been called by him, listened to his teachings, even seen him perform miracles. But they've not yet answered with absolute certainty this crucial question we all wrestle with at some point: "Is he really, truly God in every moment of my life?"

It's the question we ask ourselves when the storms of life come. Anxiety will tell us the answer is no. The boat is sinking, and we're in charge of saving ourselves. There is no hope; the rain will never end. No one cares about us. This is the end.

But the Spirit within us whispers yes! God is not distant; he's in the boat with us. No matter how the storm rages, he will not let us drown in our difficulties. He is present and powerful, and he cares about every detail of our lives.

The disciples experienced the complete calming of a physical storm. This side of heaven, the emotional storms we're in may not fully go away. The depression may come back. The panic attack might not stop instantly. The stress in our job could continue. Sometimes the storms calm, and sometimes we find calm in the storm because we know with certainty these two things: God is God in every moment of our lives, and with him, we can make it through anything.

. . . .

God, when storms come, I pray for your supernatural calm, either by causing the storm to cease or by giving me hope, strength, and inner stillness in the middle of it. You are God in every moment of my life. Amen.

What's a storm you've faced? How did you experience God's presence and peace in it?

THIRTY-SIX

God Invites You to Stop Striving

> But the Lord said to her, "My dear Martha, you are worried and upset over all these details! There is only one thing worth being concerned about. Mary has discovered it, and it will not be taken away from her."
>
> Luke 10:41–42

Martha's hands are covered in flour, and she runs through her mental to-do list again as she kneads the dough. "Mary," she asks, "can you get the olive oil?" But silence is the only answer, and she turns to see an empty kitchen. *Where is Mary?* It's a familiar question to Martha. She heard it from her parents while she and Mary were growing up, as she was the older sister and was expected to look out for her younger sibling. Mary might have been up a tree, chasing a stray dog, or picking wildflowers. Wherever she was, whatever she did, Martha was supposed to take care of her.

Mary the dreamer.

Martha the doer.

Mary the romantic.

Martha the responsible one.

"Mary!" she says again in what her sister calls her "bossy voice." She wipes her hands on her apron and goes to find her sister. When she enters the room full of guests, she sees Mary at the feet of Jesus doing nothing.

Enough is enough. "Lord, doesn't it seem unfair to you that my sister just sits here while I do all the work? Tell her to come and help me" (Luke 10:40). Jesus's response is not what Martha expects. "My dear Martha, you are worried and upset over all these details! There is only one thing worth being concerned about. Mary has discovered it, and it will not be taken away from her" (vv. 41–42).

Jesus looks at Martha as he says these words in a way that makes her feel deep in her soul that *he knows*. He knows how hard she has tried. He knows the pressure she's felt to always be the "good" one. He sees the weight of responsibility that's so heavy on her shoulders. He understands that she is anxious and so tired, so very tired, that all she wants to do is sit down too. His words could have felt like a rebuke, but, instead, they're a long-overdue release.

149

No one knows the exact details of this scene from Scripture, but as a counselor, life coach, and fellow human being, I can easily imagine it unfolding this way. Why? Because all of us take on roles in childhood that shape our behavior in adulthood. (By the way, Mary isn't exempt—she has a role that needs healing too. It just shows up later.) We pick up these roles because they serve a purpose, but then we forget to lay them down when they've outlived their usefulness. Jesus is giving Martha that opportunity.

In this story, we see Martha striving, overwhelmed, and acting as if it all depends on her. But later when Jesus arrives after her brother, Lazarus, has died, there's a noticeable shift. The first thing Martha says to Jesus is, "Lord, if only you had been here, my brother would not have died. But even now I know that God will give you whatever you ask" (John 11:21–22).

What's the difference? When Martha tries to recruit Jesus to rebuke Mary, she is striving for control—of dinner, of her sister, and of even Jesus. She's the bossy older sister. But this time her actions and words express this: *Jesus, you are in control.* She's embraced her identity as the beloved daughter of God.

Anxiety tells all of us, but especially those of us who took on a lot of responsibility in childhood, "You can have control." We want our loved ones safe, the dinner to be perfect, and everything to turn out the way we'd hope. But life is unpredictable, mistakes happen, hearts and dishes get broken. What we need more than control is to know that someone else is in charge of everything, that he is good and he loves us. We think control will give us invincibility, but what we really need— the "one thing worth being concerned about" (Luke 10:42)—is intimacy with Someone who will take care of us no matter what happens.

....

God, you've been with me every moment of my life. You know the roles I may have stepped into that you never intended for me. When they cause me to strive and stress out, please reveal the true source of my anxiety and set me free. Amen.

What was your role in your family—the responsible one, the rebel, something else? What's a role God has given you instead (example: beloved daughter)?

THIRTY-SEVEN

God Knows How It Feels

He became anguished and distressed. He told them, "My soul is crushed with grief to the point of death. Stay here and keep watch with me."

Matthew 26:37–38

Jesus knows the cross is coming when he rides a donkey into Jerusalem and the crowd praises him, when he serves wine and bread to his disciples at the last supper, even as he washes their feet. His first cry was as a baby in a manger, and his last will be as the Savior on a cross. But he still experiences inner conflict over this assignment from God. He goes to the garden of Gethsemane to pray and becomes "anguished and distressed," which sounds a lot like anxiety (Matt. 26:37).

This brings up a question: Is anxiety sin? Many of us have been told, whether directly or indirectly, that it is. I've felt deep shame and guilt because I continued to experience anxiety even though I prayed and obeyed.

Yet here we see Jesus doing the same. How can that be? I think we've believed a distortion of God's intent about anxiety. Verses like Philippians 4:6 say, "Do not be anxious" (NIV), and we interpret them as, "Don't ever experience any anxiety at all or you don't have faith."

But we need to understand there are two kinds of anxiety: physical and psychological. Our biological anxiety response is activated when our brains perceive a threat. This threat can be tangible (like a bear charging at us or the knowledge we're about to be crucified). In today's world, it's more likely psychological—something emotional or social. When this response gets triggered, the adrenaline that's released causes biological reactions like a racing heart, rapid breathing, shaking hands, or sweating. Our mind also goes into threat-assessment mode, which means we imagine worst-case scenarios. The fight-or-flight response is automatic, not optional.

Psychological anxiety is about our hearts, minds, and souls. Philippians 4:6 doesn't stop with "do not be anxious." It continues, "But in every situation, by prayer and petition, with thanksgiving, present your requests to God. And the peace of God, which transcends all understanding, will guard your hearts and your minds in Christ Jesus" (vv. 6–7 NIV). This is what we see Jesus doing. In a time of deep anxiety, he prays and petitions, "My Father! If it is possible, let this cup of suffering be taken away from me. Yet I want your will to be done, not mine" (Matt. 26:39). He battles anxiety, takes it to God, and chooses to obey anyway.

When Jesus is betrayed, arrested, falsely accused, and forced to carry his cross, a supernatural peace sustains him. It's interesting that Philippians says this peace will guard our hearts and minds, but it doesn't mention our bodies. The reality is that our hands might still shake, our knees may knock, and our hearts could pound. Jesus was so distressed in Gethsemane that Luke, a disciple and doctor, wrote in his Gospel that Jesus experienced hematohidrosis (sweating blood).

It's okay if your physical anxiety never fully goes away. Yes, it would be wonderful if your anxiety disappeared. And if you're having symptoms like panic attacks that interfere with your everyday life, then please get help. But you're not in trouble with God for how your body is responding. It doesn't mean you're spiritually failing; it means you're a human doing hard, courageous things.

And Jesus knows exactly what that feels like.

....

God, thank you for coming to earth and living in a human body. It's such a relief and gift to know you understand how that can be a challenge sometimes. Give me the courage and strength to obey you rather than my anxiety today. Amen.

What have you been taught about anxiety that might not be true, like that you're never allowed to experience it? What do you now know is true?

THIRTY-EIGHT

God Can Heal in Many Ways

Jesus told him, "Stand up, pick up your mat, and walk!"

John 5:8

The man lies next to the pool of Bethesda, as he does each day. Jews say an angel stirs the waters and whoever enters them first will be healed. The Greeks who worship Asclepius, the god of healing, say a spirit is responsible. After thirty-eight years of illness, the man no longer cares who's right. He actually doesn't care about much at all. Life is monotonous, one day blending into the next, sleeping, waking, sitting—but never walking.

He's become used to feeling invisible, unworthy, overlooked. So it startles him when an unfamiliar voice asks him an unexpected question: "Would you like to get well?" (John 5:6). Years ago, he might have answered with a resounding yes. But time has worn down his hope until he finally surrenders the last of it. He says, "I can't, sir . . . for I have no one to put me into the pool when the water bubbles up. Someone else always gets there ahead of me" (v. 7).

The man believes healing can come to him in only one way. But Jesus blows that away and tells him, "Stand up, pick up your mat, and walk!" (v. 8). The man jumps to his feet on legs that are suddenly strong, lifts his mat with arms long unused, and takes his first steps toward a completely different future.

When we deal with anxiety for years, we can become fixated on one way we believe we'll be healed too.

If I just pray enough . . .

If I do one more Bible study . . .

If I can find the perfect church . . .

Like the Jews and Greeks told people the pool of Bethesda could heal them, a religious expert might have told us a certain spiritual solution will magically cure our anxiety. We try hard to make the advice we're given work, but we never quite seem to get there. We become stuck like the man by the pool, hope slipping away as we keep waiting for "someday."

But we serve a God who is limitless, who heals in so many different ways. God has used wise counselors to help my mind heal. He has provided gifted doctors and medicine created by brilliant scientists to help my nervous system heal. He has enabled me to release stress through exercise in ways that help my body heal. He has sent caring friends and family to help my heart heal. He has given me prayer and his Word and his love to help my soul heal. All these combined have made a huge difference in my anxiety.

Sometimes we're told God can use miracles, but not medicine; preachers, but not doctors; Scripture, but not a good night's sleep. But "whatever is good and perfect is a gift coming down to us from God our Father" (James 1:17) and "the earth is the Lord's, and everything in it. The world and all its people belong to him" (Ps. 24:1).

Jesus might be asking us today, "Do you want to get well?" Perhaps we've tried so hard for so long to make one way work that we're tempted to say, "I can't." If so, this is the moment where we can choose to believe more is possible than we may have imagined. We can say, "Yes, Jesus, show me how you want to work in my life today, even if it's not at all what I expected."

....

God, you are a limitless healer, and I open myself up to whoever and whatever you want to use to help my anxiety. You care about every part of who I am—heart, soul, mind, and body. I entrust all of me to you. Amen.

Think of all the things that help with your anxiety and thank God for each one.

THIRTY-NINE

God Frees You from Fear

The jailer called for lights and ran to the dungeon and fell down trembling before Paul and Silas. Then he brought them out and asked, "Sirs, what must I do to be saved?"

Acts 16:29–30

Don't fall asleep, don't fall asleep," the jailer repeats to himself in the darkness of the dungeon. Not only could he face severe punishment for sleeping on the job, but every time he drifts off, he has nightmares about what he's seen and done in this place. He can hear two prisoners singing hymns and praying. Why does it calm his tortured mind? His eyes close.

The next thing he knows, the ground beneath him is shaking. Where is he? What is happening? He reaches for his sword, then sees the prison doors wide open. This is no nightmare. The prisoners have escaped, he's

160

failed, and he knows his fate. He could end his life before the brutal Romans take it. He pauses. Is he really ready to die?

He hears a voice. "Stop! Don't kill yourself. We are all here!" (Acts 16:28). It's one of the men who'd been singing and praying. What kind of man would stay in prison when he could go free? *The kind who has peace even in a dungeon*, he thinks. Suddenly he desperately wants that too. The jailer rushes to the dungeon and falls down trembling before Paul and Silas. Then he brings them out and asks, "Sirs, what must I do to be saved?" (v. 30).

Fear can have an interesting side effect. It reminds us of our need for God. Turbulence shakes the plane, and suddenly everyone is praying. Tragedy strikes, and a family who's been out of church for years calls a preacher. An unnamed chaplain is reported to have said at the service for a fallen soldier during World War I, "We have no atheists in the trenches."

I don't believe God causes fear to make us depend on him more. That would be contrary to his character. I think, instead, it's simply that we, as humans, have a tendency to live independently, and fear-provoking moments remind us that this is not the best plan. Our everyday experiences of fear aren't likely to be as intense as the jailer's or on the scale of a world war. But we can still shift our perspective to see fear as a prompt to reach out to God.

I work with writers as a life coach, and a question they often ask is, "When will I completely stop being afraid?" I always say, "You won't. Fear is part of doing brave, hard things." Then I tell them that the day I wake up and say, "I've totally got this figured out. I feel absolutely no fear," I should walk away. Because that's when I'm most likely to believe that I can do on my own what God has called me to do.

Fear keeps us humble. It reminds us that we are small. It lets us see our inadequacy. It reveals the temporary nature of all that surrounds us. This is exceedingly uncomfortable. But it can also be a neon arrow pointing us to God.

Paul and Silas told the jailer all he needed to do was believe in Jesus, and he joyfully did so. At midnight he thought life was over, but by dawn he brought Paul and Silas "into his house and set a meal before them, and he and his entire household rejoiced because they all believed in God" (v. 34).

From fear to faith.

From ending a life to beginning a new one.

From isolation to celebration.

From prison to new freedom.

God changes everything.

....

God, you are the one who sets my heart free from fear. When I'm afraid, help me see that fear as a reminder to reach out to you for help. Amen.

How does your fear remind you of your need for God?

FORTY

God's Love Is Given, Not Earned

And I am convinced that nothing can ever separate us from God's love. Neither death nor life, neither angels nor demons, neither our fears for today nor our worries about tomorrow—not even the powers of hell can separate us from God's love.

Romans 8:38

Saul wonders, *What can I do to earn God's approval?* As a Pharisee, he strives each day to keep the 613 laws required of him. But it still doesn't feel like enough. So he takes his zeal to the next level, asking authorities for permission to bring followers of "The Way" back to Jerusalem in chains.

But God has different plans for Saul. As he nears Damascus, a light shines from heaven and a voice says, "I am Jesus, the one you are persecuting!" (Acts 9:5). Saul becomes the apostle Paul and eventually writes most of the New Testament, including the book of Romans.

Those of us who struggle with anxiety may also find ourselves asking, "What can I do to earn God's approval?" This doesn't mean we are Pharisees, but it may indicate we've been part of a religious system that has Pharisaical characteristics like these:

- Your worth comes from your works.
- Image is more important than intimacy with God.
- Rules are emphasized more than relationship.
- Guilt and fear are used to motivate people.
- The world is divided into "us" and "them."
- Those who mess up are shamed and excluded.

I grew up in a church setting that leaned toward legalism. While I'm grateful for many parts of my spiritual history, I've also come to see that elements of it contributed to my anxiety. Even as a kid I often worried, "Is God mad at me?" I did my best to keep all the "rules," but inevitably, I fell short. Then the critical voice in my head would kick in, and I'd anxiously try even harder to earn God's approval. Can you relate?

If so, Paul's words are good news. As a former Pharisee, what he writes in Romans 8 is scandalous. He spent his entire life trying to be perfect and now says all we need is God's perfect love. For those of us who have spent our entire lives trying to earn God's approval, this is the answer our souls need.

I want you to read this verse with your name inserted. "I am convinced that nothing can ever separate (your name) from God's love. Neither death nor life, neither angels nor demons, neither our fears for today nor (your name's) worries about tomorrow—not even the powers of hell can separate (your name) from God's love" (Rom. 8:38).

When anxiety tries to tell you God's love is conditional or you must earn his approval, when you hear the echoes of the voices of the Pharisees in your life, cling to this truth: Nothing can separate you from God's love—no exceptions. No mistake or shortcoming, no weakness or struggle, no relapse or rule broken. Not even that secret you've never told anyone. Not that battle you lost again yesterday. Not the critical voice in your mind.

You never have to ask, "What can I do to earn God's approval?" because his love is a gift and his grace is a certainty you can count on for all eternity.

....

God, thank you that nothing can ever separate me from your love. When my anxiety tries to tell me that's not true, draw me back to your grace. Amen.

What do you worry will separate you from God's love? Finish this sentence with it: "Nothing can ever separate me from God's love, not even _____."

FORTY-ONE

God Will Renew Your Mind

Don't copy the behavior and customs of this world, but let God transform you into a new person by changing the way you think. Then you will learn to know God's will for you, which is good and pleasing and perfect.

Romans 12:2

While modern life has new threats, the power of fear over humanity has existed from the beginning. In the apostle Paul's time, Roman officials published a daily gazette called the *Acta Diurna*. Notices and news were posted in public places. The purpose wasn't merely information; it was intimidation and control.

Much of the news we consume today is also fear based. Why? Fear commands attention, and your attention is what newsmakers are selling to advertisers.

Journalist Martin Lindstrom says, "Clearly, fear is a powerful persuader, and you'd better believe that marketers and advertisers know it and aren't afraid to exploit it to the fullest."[1]

But aren't newsmakers required to be fair? Not anymore. In 1987, the FCC Fairness Doctrine requiring newsmakers to be unbiased was repealed. Since then, news has shifted from public service to an opportunity for commercial gain. Yes, there are still people in the industry who truly want to help the public, but we need to be wise about what we see, hear, and share.

When Paul says, "Don't copy the behaviors and customs of this world" (Rom. 12:2), it's easy to imagine a wild party in Las Vegas. But on a deeper level, if we live in a culture motivated by fear, then changing the way we think means learning to be motivated instead by faith.

One way we can do this is by noticing how the news we consume affects us. Does what we're reading, watching, or hearing cause us to experience fear? Who is the source, and do they have an agenda? Is what's being shared actually true and/or as dire as it seems? Even if it *is* true, where will we put our trust—in newsmakers or in the Maker of heaven and earth?

If something or someone on the news or social media consistently evokes anxiety in you, especially in a way that makes you feel helpless, consider minimizing or eliminating that voice in your life. It's okay to set boundaries around how much news you consume. It's okay to unfollow someone on social media. It's okay to seek sources that give you courage rather than try to make you conform.

When we start living out of faith rather than fear, it may feel strange at first. We'll likely have thoughts such as, *What if I miss something important?* or *Something bad will happen if I don't know everything.* When we've operated in fear for a long time, it literally forms neural pathways in our minds. As we change how we think, the way Paul encourages us to do, our brains actually make new pathways. True transformation takes persistence and perseverance.

When you feel anxiety rising and want to turn on the TV or reach for your phone to check just one more headline, pause, take a deep breath, and say, "Not this time, fear. With God's help, I'm renewing my mind."

....

God, you know everything that has ever happened in this world and my life. Help me consume news in ways that lead to more peace in my heart instead of having the news consume me. Amen.

What are your sources for news? What boundaries do you need to make sure news doesn't increase your anxiety?

FORTY-TWO

God Shows Up in Your Awkward Moments

I came to you in weakness—timid and trembling. And my message and my preaching were very plain. Rather than using clever and persuasive speeches, I relied only on the power of the Holy Spirit. I did this so you would trust not in human wisdom but in the power of God.

1 Corinthians 2:3–5

The apostle Paul has an impressive spiritual résumé: circumcised on the eighth day, as Jewish law requires; a citizen of Israel; part of the tribe of Benjamin; a Pharisee and religious leader. Then a man who has an intimate encounter with Jesus, hears the actual voice of God, and is entrusted to share the gospel with the gentiles. Why would he ever be anxious or awkward?

Yet he tells the Corinthian church, "I came to you in weakness—timid and trembling" (1 Cor. 2:3). We're not used to hearing this from modern spiritual leaders. In our world, charisma, high energy, a big personality, and smooth delivery are often the expectations. Because of that, we believe this lie: *if my anxiety shows, God can't use me.*

But Paul says that our weakness can actually point people to the power of God. He may also have come timid and trembling for another reason; Paul wanted the Corinthians to trust him. Before becoming a believer, he persecuted, threatened, and was eager to kill Christians. After his conversion when he "arrived in Jerusalem, he tried to meet with the believers, but they were all afraid of him. They did not believe he had truly become a believer!" (Acts 9:26).

Sweating, stuttering, blushing, or other signs of social nervousness can actually make others see us as more trustworthy and likable. Mark Leary, psychology professor and director of the Interdisciplinary Behavioral Research Center at Duke University, explains that responses like these are "necessary to signal that I care what you think about me."[1] About people who never express such responses, he says, "You couldn't trust them. They're not sensitive to what other people think."[2]

Psychologist Barbara Markway agrees with this perspective on awkwardness. "We think that people are going to reject us, but it can be endearing," she says.[3]

Others feel nervous and insecure too. When our discomfort shows, we're expressing two things: "You matter to me" and "You're not the only one." As we embrace our humanness, we give those around us permission to do the same.

I once did a workshop at a conference, and halfway through my computer stopped working. I couldn't use any of my slides. At first, I felt flustered (and it showed), but I finally took a deep breath and said, "I'm glad you're seeing this. Because at some point, something like this will happen to you too. And it will be okay. God can use you anyway." At the end of the conference, a woman walked up to me and said, "The most helpful thing for me out of this whole weekend was seeing you mess up. Now I know it's okay if I do too."

The Corinthians didn't need to see Paul give a perfect performance. They needed to see he had been transformed by Jesus. It's okay if sometimes our anxiety shows. Those might unexpectedly be the moments when God shows most in us too.

....

God, thank you that I don't have to be perfect for you to use me. I can even be timid and trembling. Give me the courage not to hold back until I have it all together, but to show up as I am—to you be all the glory. Amen.

When have you felt nervous and the situation worked out anyway?

FORTY-THREE

God Clears the Clutter in Your Life

For God is not a God of disorder but of peace.

1 Corinthians 14:33

When Paul wrote to the Corinthians, they were a new church full of energy and enthusiasm. This led to chaotic services, people talking over each other, interruptions, and confusion. Paul urges these believers to bring order to their meetings. Why? Because it reflects God's character.

In the beginning, God *created*. We see his imagination in pink flamingos, orange starfish, the taste of strawberry ice cream, and the thrill of a first kiss. But he also methodically made the world over seven days, one step at a time, by intentional design.

We, as humans created in his image, crave order. Writer Anne-Marie Gambelin explains,

176

Clutter can trigger the release of the stress hormone cortisol, which can increase tension and anxiety and lead to unhealthy habits. Cortisol is a hormone produced in response to stress by the hypothalamus-pituitary-adrenal axis (HPA). Chronic clutter can create prolonged stress, throwing us into a state of low-grade, perpetual fight-or-flight—the system designed to help us survive.[1]

We often think of clutter only in terms of extra items in our home, but there are multiple forms. In the Corinthian church, there was sound clutter. In modern times, we can experience something similar because of all the sound notifications we receive through our phones. There's also visual clutter, like when our house is always messy or the stacks of paper on our desk drive us crazy. We can also have time clutter, which happens when our schedules become too full. Financial clutter means we have extra expenses that consume resources but don't add to the quality of our lives. Emotional clutter happens when we collect hurts but never take time to deal with them.

When we're feeling anxious and can't understand why, one of the most helpful questions we can ask ourselves is, "Where do I have clutter in my life?" Once we identify the source, we can start bringing order to that area again. This might mean clearing off a counter (tidying has actually been shown to have a calming effect).

We might need to turn our phone to silent for a few hours. Maybe we cross a commitment off our calendar. Perhaps it's time to make an appointment with a counselor to work through the thoughts and emotions filling up our mind and heart.

In her book *Outer Order, Inner Calm*, Gretchen Rubin says this about clutter: "By getting rid of the things I don't use, don't need, or don't love, as well as the things that don't work, don't fit, or don't suit, I free my mind—and my shelves—for what I truly value. And that's true for most people."[2] She's talking about physical clutter, but we can apply this principle to any area of our lives that's causing us anxiety.

Sometimes what stresses us out isn't bad; it's actually just too much of what's good. For the Corinthians, having so many people who wanted to prophesy showed the church was vibrant and alive. But without order, it led to confusion and overwhelm and became an unhelpful distraction. Sometimes less really is more.

....

God, reveal any clutter in my life that's causing my anxiety. Then show me what I need to let go of so I can be free and live with greater peace today. Amen.

What's cluttering your heart, mind, life, or home right now? How could that be adding to your anxiety? What's one small way you can clear a little clutter today?

FORTY-FOUR

God Is Strong in Our Weakness

Three different times I begged the Lord to take it away. Each time he said, "My grace is all you need. My power works best in weakness." So now I am glad to boast about my weaknesses, so that the power of Christ can work through me.

2 Corinthians 12:8–9

The apostle Paul never shares specifics about the "thorn in my flesh" that he begs God to take away. But those of us who struggle with anxiety can relate to having something in our lives we wish would disappear completely. I've asked God many times to free me fully from my anxiety, but that hasn't happened yet.

I believe one reason is because my anxiety is tied to so many of my God-given strengths. That may sound strange, but researchers have found those who struggle with anxiety also often have the following strengths:

- empathy
- diligence
- responsibility
- attention to detail
- self-awareness
- resilience
- courage
- compassion

The brain and nervous system wiring that makes some of us more vulnerable to anxiety also comes with powerful gifts our world needs. I often talk about the core parts of who we are as being on a continuum like this one.

My Nervous System

Anxiety (Struggle) ————————————— Empathy (Strength)

God intentionally designed us, so he's not interested in "taking away" parts of who we are. Instead, he wants us to move from the struggle side of this continuum to the strength side.

How does this happen? God told Paul, "My grace is all you need" (2 Cor. 12:9). The first step is letting go of guilt and shame over our struggles, because that only causes us to stay stuck. Instead, we can embrace the freedom of God's abundant grace. Then God said, "My power works best in weakness" (v. 9). This means we don't have to "fix" ourselves. We're invited to bring our struggles to God and ask for his help.

I believe we're to be proactive partners in the process as well. To help my anxiety, I've learned I need spiritual practices like prayer, physical rhythms like rest and exercise, and social support from those who love me. Each of these helps me align with how God created me to live and moves me toward the strength end of the continuum.

God created each of us in an amazing and wonderful way. Because we live in a fallen world, we each have potential struggles and powerful strengths. Yes, anxiety can feel like a thorn in our flesh. But sometimes thorns come with beautiful things. As a quote often attributed to author Henry Van Dyke says, "The best rosebush, after all, is not that which has the fewest thorns, but that which bears the finest roses."

....

God, I choose to believe you made me in an amazing and wonderful way, even if I don't always feel like it. Help me embrace who I am and become all you've created me to be a little more each day. Amen.

What part of who you are do you sometimes struggle with? How could it actually be the other end of a God-given strength (example: anxiety/empathy, anger/passion, perfectionism/attention to detail)?

FORTY-FIVE

God Overpowers Perfectionism

So Christ has truly set us free. Now make sure that you
stay free, and don't get tied up again in slavery to the law.

Galatians 5:1

Paul, home from his first missionary journey, listens
to the latest update on the church in Galatia.
After his departure, Judaizers came in and told the
people that simply believing in Jesus wasn't enough—
they needed to follow the Jewish law too. As a
former Pharisee, Paul knows the heaviness of this burden and the power of being set free. His words
in Galatians reflect his passion for God's people not
to fall back into following rules rather than living in
faith.

I used to read Galatians and think I couldn't
really relate. I didn't feel tempted to follow the Old

Testament law. Leviticus was my least favorite book in the Bible (you too?). But one day I realized *perfectionism was my own modern version of living under the law*. At its core, perfectionism is the belief that if we're not perfect, then something bad will happen. It's a reward/punishment system. If I perform well, I get approval from God and others. If I don't, I get rejection and shame. This is not a system based on grace.

How does perfectionism relate to anxiety? The brains of perfectionists perceive imperfection as a threat, which can activate our amygdala (the area in charge of our fight-or-flight response). So when we think we don't meet the expectations (laws) of God, others, or ourselves, we experience anxiety.

How do we identify our personal laws? We can start by looking for words like *shall*, *should*, *must*, *have to*. Here are a few of my personal commandments of perfectionism:

- Thou shall make everyone like you.
- Thou shall not make mistakes.
- Thou shall get it right the first time.
- Thou shall never get angry.

The law is whatever we're trusting in to gain approval and affection. Sometimes the laws we follow come from authority figures in our childhood. *Thou shall never make the family look bad.* Sometimes they come from religious organizations. *Thou shall be at church every time the doors are open.* We can pick them up from the culture around us. *Thou shall never age.* Or we might go through trauma that makes them seem necessary for our survival. *Thou shall not trust anyone ever again.* Our anxiety throws laws at us all the time. *Thou shall never mess up in public.*

God doesn't condemn us for these laws. Quite the opposite, he's still in the business of setting perfectionists free. Paul asks the Galatians, "After starting your new lives in the Spirit, why are you now trying to become perfect by your own human effort?" (Gal. 3:3). My first answer to that question would be *fear.*

Fear of rejection.

Fear of looking foolish.

Fear of letting people down.

Fear of disappointing God.

But because of Jesus, we no longer have to earn approval, hustle for love, prove our worth, or try to be good enough for God. We are no longer under any law; we are under grace. Perfectionism has lost its power over us. "Christ has truly set us free" (5:1).

....

God, thank you for setting me free from fear, perfectionism, and living under the law. Help me fully embrace your grace. Amen.

What are some of your personal commandments? What is the truth God wants to replace them with today?

FORTY-SIX

God Gives You Armor for Anxiety

Be strong in the Lord and in his mighty power. Put on the full armor of God, so that you can take your stand against the devil's schemes.

Ephesians 6:10–11 NIV

Great is Artemis of the Ephesians!" The rioters' shouts echoed off the walls of the amphitheater. Paul caught a glimpse of Demetrius, a silversmith who made his living creating shrines for Artemis and employed many craftsmen in the city. Demetrius incited the crowd by saying not only would Paul's preaching lead to a loss of wealth, but their great goddess Artemis would also be disrespected and dismissed. Paul tried to enter the amphitheater, but his companions held him back and said, "It's too dangerous."

Artemis was a Greek goddess associated with the hunt, and her symbols included a knife, bow, and arrow. So when Paul, home from his third missionary journey, writes to the Ephesians, it makes sense that he includes the imagery of armor. Most of us have heard of the armor of God, but how can we use it in our battle with anxiety? Let's walk through the pieces of it together.

"Stand firm then, with the belt of truth buckled around your waist" (Eph. 6:14 NIV). The belt described here, the kind worn by a Roman soldier, would have been eight to twelve inches tall and made of thick leather. It covered much of a soldier's torso, offering not only protection but also security and stability. It was the first piece of armor to be put on and held many of the others together. Truth protects us from the lies anxiety tries to tell us.

"With the breastplate of righteousness in place" (v. 14 NIV). Covering the chest was not a matter of personal preference—it was about life and death. The breastplate (also known as body armor) protected the vital organs, especially the heart. In some instances, it was literally called a "heart guard." The righteousness of Christ imparted to us through what he did on the cross guards our hearts.

"With your feet fitted with the readiness that comes from the gospel of peace" (v. 15 NIV). Soldiers wore leather sandals that had small spikes attached to the soles, similar to soccer cleats. These shoes allowed them to hold their ground when the enemy attacked. When anxiety comes at us, we can stand in peace.

"Take up the shield of faith" (v. 16 NIV). The shield itself was made out of wood (like the cross), covered by animal skins (a reminder of sacrifice, God gave his Son for us), and the leather of the shield was frequently rubbed down with oil (which brings to mind the anointing of the Holy Spirit). We can stand behind our faith in vulnerable moments when anxiety is likely to strike.

"Take the helmet of salvation and the sword of the Spirit, which is the word of God" (v. 17 NIV). The helmet is designed to protect our minds, which is where worry tries to take hold. The sword of the Spirit is the only both offensive and defensive weapon in our armor. It's the key to not just protecting ourselves but proactively going after anything that tries to steal our peace.

When we start to feel anxious, one strategy is to pause and pray through the armor of God, putting it on from head to toe. We're in an invisible battle, but we serve an invincible God—and with him we are mightier than we know.

....

God, thank you for giving me the armor I need to fight my battles. With you, I am not a worrier but a warrior, and anxiety will not win. Amen.

What piece of the armor of God do you need most today? Why?

FORTY-SEVEN

God Will Help You Fight for Peace

Don't worry about anything; instead, pray about everything. Tell God what you need, and thank him for all he has done. Then you will experience God's peace, which exceeds anything we can understand. His peace will guard your hearts and minds as you live in Christ Jesus.

Philippians 4:6–7

The apostle Paul thought of the Philippian believers with great affection. He wrote to them not as a rebuke but as a reminder of his love for them and with encouragement for how to keep growing in faith. The warmth of Paul's words makes it easy to picture him writing them from somewhere safe, like at his kitchen table after a good meal. But he actually wrote to the Philippians from a Roman prison near the end of his life.

Prisons during this time were known for their terrible conditions: "Unbearable cold, lack of water, cramped quarters, and sickening stench from few toilets made sleeping difficult and waking hours miserable."[1] When Paul wrote, "Don't worry about anything" (Phil. 4:6), he had *plenty* of reasons to worry. Picture him leaning against the wall of a dark cell, chains on his hands and feet, closing his eyes to tell God what he needs and thank him for all he has done. Imagine Paul glancing at a guard pacing through the prison and telling the Philippians, "His peace will guard your hearts and minds" (v. 7). What kind of peace is this? Paul himself says it "exceeds anything we can understand" (v. 7).

Mark and I went through almost a decade of infertility. At times it felt like a dark place where we were trapped, unable to move forward with our dreams. I cried in bathrooms, asked God questions, experienced confusion and frustration. Yet over time, I began to experience what Paul describes—a peace beyond what I could understand.

It's easy to think peace is something that will simply descend on us the first time we ask for God's help. But in my experience, it's something we fight for over and over. Thankfully, Paul gives us a battle plan.

Don't worry about anything.

Pray about everything.

Tell God what you need.

Thank him for all he has done.

Repeat, repeat, repeat.

Is this easy? Absolutely not. Will there be times when we *do* worry, even feel despair? Yes, we are human, after all. Will we experience resistance? Every day.

But we are not alone in the fight. And, over time, the battle will get less intense. When I first started healing from our struggle with infertility, having peace felt like hand-to-hand combat. Intense. Personal. Continual. Over time it started to feel more like the enemy would occasionally toss a grenade my way that I had to defuse. I could sense God guarding my heart and mind, protecting the peace I'd fought so hard to attain.

When people asked me how I was doing, I started saying, "I have a peace about it." If they looked at me with disbelief, I'd add, "It's not a cliché. It's the kind of peace that comes after war."

If you have to fight for peace, nothing is wrong with your faith. There is peace that comes from the absence of all pain or difficulty. But there is a deeper, more powerful peace that comes after the heat of battle. This is the kind of peace only warriors know.

Fight on.

....

God, when peace requires a battle, give me the strength to fight. I'm so glad to know you're with me and you will guard my heart and mind. Amen.

Go through the steps Paul provides with a situation in your life right now.

Don't worry about anything.

Pray about everything.

Tell God what you need.

Thank him for all he has done.

FORTY-EIGHT

God Will Help You Retrain Your Brain

Fix your thoughts on what is true, and honorable, and right, and pure, and lovely, and admirable. Think about things that are excellent and worthy of praise.

Philippians 4:8

Fix your thoughts . . ." When the apostle Paul wrote these words, he didn't mean to repair what's broken. Instead, *fix* here means to focus our thoughts in a consistent, intentional way.

We all know what it's like to feel as though our minds are all over the place, jumping from one thought to another. We also have a negativity bias, which means we naturally notice what's wrong more than what's right in our lives. This helps with our survival; if a bear came charging into the coffee shop where I'm working, I'd notice it. But left unchecked, our negativity bias means our thoughts drift toward the opposite of what Paul said.

So how do we retrain our brains? One simple way is through visualization. Think of the last time you worried. Maybe you pictured a loved one getting in a car wreck, losing your job, or a doctor sharing a terrible diagnosis with you. If you've ever had thoughts like these, you *already* visualize. To visualize simply means to picture something in our minds. What helps with anxiety is learning to do so in constructive rather than destructive ways.

Visualization is powerful because of the way God created our brains. Neuropsychologist Amy Palmer explains, "The brain has the same activity when it visualizes doing an action as it does when it is physically performing the action."[1] (This is why anxiety can be so harmful to our health and happiness; our brains and bodies react as if the terrible things we imagine are actually happening to us.)

Visualization also engages the reticular activating system (RAS), an area of our brains that acts as a filter. Our RAS determines what we pay attention to, and it naturally prioritizes two things: threats and what we tell it is relevant. For example, if you ever decide to shop for a new red car, then you'll likely start seeing red cars everywhere. Were they there before? Of course, but your RAS labeled them as irrelevant, so you didn't really notice them like you do now.

When we visualize, it tells our RAS what we want it to notice. So if we practice picturing what is true, honorable, right, pure, lovely, excellent, and worthy of praise, then we will start having fewer negative thoughts.

Every morning I spend a few minutes visualizing a room full of people I love. I walk around and give each one a hug. Sometimes I picture Jesus in the room too. I engage all my senses—what do I see, hear, smell, touch, even taste? The more details I can add, the more my brain will engage. This exercise reminds me that everything I do that day is really about loving God, others, and myself. It helps me live from a place of belonging and grace, which also significantly decreases my anxiety.

If I find myself getting anxious later in the day, I sometimes do a second visualization. I pause and picture myself on the beach where we often go for vacation, my favorite place in the world. I see the waves, hear the seagulls, smell the sea, feel the sand beneath my feet, and taste the salty air on my lips. As I imagine sitting on the beach, I go through the alphabet and say a name of God for each letter. This helps me remember that no matter what happens, I'll be okay because God is good, and he's taking care of not only me but the whole world too.

Ask God for scenes that will realign your thoughts, calm your mind, and draw you closer to him. *What we focus on, we will go toward in life.* We can drift into negativity or intentionally redirect our thoughts to what is life-giving, heart-freeing, and true.

....

God, you have given me a powerful mind. Help me focus on what is true, honorable, right, pure, lovely, excellent, and worthy of praise today. Amen.

Find a quiet place where you can sit upright, and start a timer for five minutes. Begin by taking a few deep breaths—in through your nose and out through your mouth. Then picture a scene that brings you joy. It can be a memory, future hope, or something you imagine (like a room full of people you love). Fix your thoughts on that scene until the timer goes off. What did you see?

FORTY-NINE

God Equips You to Handle Anything

I have learned to be content whatever the circumstances. I know what it is to be in need, and I know what it is to have plenty. I have learned the secret of being content in any and every situation, whether well fed or hungry, whether living in plenty or in want. I can do all this through him who gives me strength.

Philippians 4:11–13 NIV

When we hear the word *content*, it's easy to think of an emotional state—a baby in his mother's arms, the feeling we get relaxing on the beach, the fullness we feel after a good meal. But Paul's words offer a different perspective, one that's helpful for those of us who struggle with anxiety. He says, "I have *learned* to be content whatever the circumstances" (Phil 4:11 NIV, emphasis added). In other words, contentment isn't an emotion; it's a skill.

Knowing contentment is a skill can take the pressure off us to make ourselves feel a certain way. Instead, like all skills, living with contentment takes *practice*. In the original language, one meaning of *content* is "independent of external circumstances."[1] When we're anxious, external circumstances (or our thoughts about them) control us. So practicing contentment means taking back that control. How do we do so?

In *Feel the Fear and Do It Anyway*, Dr. Susan Jeffers says, "At the bottom of every one of your fears is simply the fear that you can't handle whatever life may bring you."[2]

I can't handle losing my job.

I can't handle getting sick.

I can't handle a loved one leaving.

I can't handle someone being mad at me.

I can't handle the latest news headline.

I can't handle my responsibilities.

I can't handle (fill in the blank with one of your fears).

Paul says, "I have learned the secret of being content in any and every situation, whether well fed or hungry, whether living in plenty or in want" (v. 12 NIV). What is his secret? Most of us have heard it many times. "I can do all this through him who gives me strength" (v. 13 NIV). But we may never have thought of those words this way. Paul is really saying, "With Jesus, I can handle anything."

With Jesus, I can handle a Roman prison.

With Jesus, I can handle hurt and hunger.

With Jesus, I can even handle death.

When anxiety starts pushing us to ask, "What if?" or imagine the worst-case scenario, Paul's secret gives us an answer. We can pause and say, "With Jesus, I can handle whatever happens." Then we can refocus on the present rather than get distracted by a fear-filled future that may never come to be.

Think back over your life and the difficulties you've already overcome. If someone had told you in advance about those, you might have said, "If that happens, I won't be able to handle it." But you had the strength you needed because God gave it to you. You've handled hard times before, and when new challenges arise, you can be confident you'll do so again.

....

God, no matter what happens, you and I will handle it together. Thank you that nothing is too much for me, because you will always give me the strength I need. Amen.

What do you tell yourself you can't handle? Based on what you've already overcome, what's the truth?

FIFTY

God Can Even Use Conflict

Is there any encouragement from belonging to Christ? Any comfort from his love? Any fellowship together in the Spirit? Are your hearts tender and compassionate? Then make me truly happy by agreeing wholeheartedly with each other, loving one another, and working together with one mind and purpose.

Philippians 2:1–2

The apostle Paul expresses concern for two kinds of peace in the lives of the Philippians: peace *within* each of them individually and peace *between* them in their relationships. Conflict is one of the most anxiety-provoking situations, and it's nothing new. Paul says, "Now I appeal to Euodia and Syntyche. Please, because you belong to the Lord, settle your disagreement" (Phil. 4:2).

Many of us have been taught that "settle your disagreement" means acting nice and pretending all is well. But that's half-hearted peace, and Paul says it will make him happy to see the Philippians "agreeing wholeheartedly" (2:2). Authors David Johnson and Jeff VanVonderen say, "Peace and unity are important in the body of Christ. But experiencing true peace and unity does not mean pretending to get along or acting like we agree when we don't."[1]

Half-hearted peace puts a smile on its face and acts like everything is fine. Wholehearted peace has the courage to speak the truth in love. Half-hearted peace holds back out of fear. Wholehearted peace bravely reaches out. Half-hearted peace talks behind someone's back. Wholehearted peace dares to have hard conversations face-to-face. Half-hearted peace leads to resentment. Wholehearted peace leads to restoration. Half-hearted peace has the goal of decreasing anxiety. Wholehearted peace has the goal of true unity.

How can we start choosing wholehearted peace in our lives? The first step is to get rid of lies we've believed about conflict.

Lie: All conflict is bad.

Truth: Conflict is a necessary part of healthy relationships.

Lie: God wants me to get along with everyone all the time.

Truth: Jesus himself didn't get along with everyone all the time.

Lie: I can't handle anyone being mad at me.

Truth: Someone being mad at me is uncomfortable but not unbearable.

Once we move past these lies, we can start practicing constructive conflict. In this kind of conflict, those involved don't insult, demean, or degrade each other. There is a clearly identified problem to be solved. The goal is not to "win" but to find a way to move forward, even if that sometimes means agreeing to disagree. Note: If someone is abusive, do not engage in conflict with them. Instead, get help from a professional, like a counselor, and create a plan for your safety.

The apostle Paul himself experienced a conflict with his dear friend and ministry partner, Barnabas. Paul wanted the two of them to go back to each city they had visited. Barnabas wanted to take John Mark with them. But Paul didn't because John Mark had previously deserted them.

"Their disagreement was so sharp that they separated" (Acts 15:39). Barnabas went to Cyprus with John Mark, and Paul went with Silas to Syria and Cilicia. This story shows us that when Paul says "agreeing wholeheartedly"

205

(Phil. 2:2), it doesn't mean giving in to what the other person wants. Instead, it means working through conflict until you find a way to move forward, even if it ultimately means you decide the best plan is to go your separate ways.

When we start pursuing wholehearted peace, our anxiety may increase short term. But as issues involving other people in our lives get resolved, it will decrease long term. Conflict causes anxiety, but sometimes it's also the best way to cure it.

. . . .

God, help me have the courage to pursue whole-hearted peace in my relationships. Give me wisdom about when and how to engage in healthy conflict. Amen.

When has conflict led to something positive in your life, even if it was hard at the time?

FIFTY-ONE

God Connects with You in Creative Ways

Since you have been raised to new life with Christ, set your sights on the realities of heaven, where Christ sits in the place of honor at God's right hand. Think about the things of heaven, not the things of earth.

Colossians 3:1–2

When Paul wrote to the Colossians, he'd not yet visited their church. He'd only heard reports that false teachers were trying to persuade new believers to go down a destructive path. Paul wrote as a protective spiritual father and mentor, reminding the Colossians to keep their faith and focus.

Anxiety can be like a "false teacher" in our lives. It tells us lies, like we're not good enough, we have to try harder, or no one will love us unless we're perfect. So how do we keep our focus on what's true?

Gary Thomas, author of *Sacred Pathways*, shares nine ways we can connect with God. While we all use each of these pathways at times, one or two usually resonate most. We can also use these sacred pathways to help with our anxiety. (Note: I've used the same titles as Thomas but adapted the descriptions based on my personal experience and studying them in more depth since I first read the book.)

Highlight or put an X by the two or three descriptions that resonate most with you.

- ☐ *Naturalists: loving God outdoors.* I feel closest to God when I'm surrounded by his creation. Anxiety tool: take a walk outside.

- ☐ *Sensates: loving God with the senses.* I feel closest to God through experiences that involve my senses, such as hearing music, tasting communion, or seeing art. Anxiety tool: create an antianxiety playlist of songs.

- ☐ *Traditionalists: loving God through ritual and symbol.* I feel closest to God through repetition and routine, such as praying in a certain way or carrying on traditions. Anxiety tool: post familiar favorite Scriptures throughout your home.

- ☐ *Ascetics: loving God in solitude and simplicity.* I feel closest to God when I can minimize external distractions and material concerns so I can lead a simple, inward-focused life. Anxiety tool: clear mental, emotional, physical, or spiritual clutter.

☐ *Activists: loving God through confrontation.* I feel closest to God when I'm confronting injustice, advocating for the oppressed, or standing up to evil. Anxiety tool: volunteer for an empowering cause.

☐ *Caregivers: loving God by loving others.* I feel closest to God through meeting the needs of others (these needs can be practical, emotional, or spiritual). Anxiety tool: ask yourself, "What's one way I can encourage someone today?"

☐ *Enthusiasts: loving God with mystery and celebration.* I feel closest to God through emotions, celebrations, and special occasions—especially those involving rejoicing and gladness. Anxiety tool: plan something joyful to do with others.

☐ *Contemplatives: loving God through adoration.* I feel closest to God through spiritual intimacy, quiet moments when I'm fully focused on my personal relationship with him. Anxiety tool: set aside time each day for quiet reflection.

☐ *Intellectuals: loving God with the mind.* I feel closest to God when I learn something new or have an aha moment that helps me grow in my understanding of him, others, and/or myself. Anxiety tool: read a helpful book.

Your top two or three descriptions are likely your most predominant sacred pathways. (You can find more detail about each in the *Sacred Pathways* book,[1] or take an online assessment at groupleaders.org/spiritual -pathways-assessment.)

If you didn't resonate with any of the sacred pathways listed, that's okay. Nine pathways feels like it leaves room for one more—yours. Pause and ask yourself, "When do I feel closest to God?" Your answer is a sacred pathway for you. Think of a way you can use that to help with your anxiety too.

....

God, I love that there are so many ways I can connect with you. When anxiety tries to be a "false teacher" in my life and take me down a destructive path, lead me toward you instead in creative ways. Amen.

Which one or two sacred pathways resonated most with you? How can you include them in your day?

FIFTY-TWO

God Takes the Pressure Off

> Make it your goal to live a quiet life, minding your own business and working with your hands, just as we instructed you before.
>
> 1 Thessalonians 4:11

*M*ake it your goal to . . .

Paul, Silas, and Timothy pause as they write to the new believers in Thessalonica. What should they give the Thessalonians as a goal? Imagine for a moment how our modern world would finish that sentence.

Make it your goal to be busy all the time.

Make it your goal to be successful and productive.

Make it your goal to look good.

Think of how some contemporary spiritual leaders might finish it too. Or how you might finish it yourself on the days when you feel not good enough.

211

Make it your goal to help everyone.

Make it your goal to change the whole world.

Make it your goal to be a spiritual hero.

What Paul, Silas, and Timothy decide to say is surprising: "Make it your goal to live a quiet life" (1 Thess. 4:11). Our anxiety can come from many sources, including goals God never intended us to pursue. When we take these on, we continually feel like we're falling short, which, of course, is anxiety provoking.

In my early twenties, I sat in a counselor's office as she drew a horizontal line across her paper. Below it, she added arrows reaching toward the line but never quite touching it. She said the horizontal line represented my expectations of myself and the arrows my actual efforts—what I could realistically do as a human.

She explained that much of my anxiety came from the gap between what I expected of myself and reality. Until I stopped putting so much pressure on myself, I would continue to experience anxiety. I wish I could say I walked out of her office and applied her wisdom right away. But it took many more years, as well as a bout of serious burnout, before I really began to ease up on myself.

Now Mark and I have 1 Thessalonians 4:11 displayed in our office. We're both entrepreneurs, and it would be easy to just keep pushing ourselves harder. We've found choosing a quiet life is far more challenging than choosing a busy, overwhelming one.

So what does a "quiet life" mean? It's easy to think it's about a *lack* of something. Fewer activities. Not as many commitments. Less noise. That can certainly be part of it, especially in seasons when we need restoration, but a quiet life is really about abiding in the presence of Someone. It's about grace silencing the voices in our minds that pressure us to do, be, and have more. In their place, we begin to experience the joy, peace, and contentment only Jesus can give.

I'll be the first to raise my hand and say this is hard for me. I'm still figuring out how to recognize when it gets loud inside. I'm practicing not proving my worth but receiving it. I'm understanding I don't need pressure to motivate me and it's okay to not meet expectations. You too?

Then let's keep learning together.

Let's remember how much we're loved.

Let's make it our goal to lead a quiet life.

....

God, you never put pressure on me. Instead, you set me free. When I start taking on goals you never intended, help me trade them for your grace. Amen.

What's one way you've been putting pressure on yourself? What does God want to say to your heart today instead?

FIFTY-THREE

God Is the Ultimate Trainer

Physical training is good, but training for godliness is much better, promising benefits in this life and in the life to come.

1 Timothy 4:8

Paul thinks back to when he first met Timothy over a decade ago. He'd just parted ways with Barnabas, one of his closest friends and encouragers. Paul traveled to Lystra in Asia Minor and heard of a young man with a reputation for strong faith. He recruited Timothy to join him on his second missionary journey before Timothy eventually became the leader of the church in Ephesus.

Scripture hints that Timothy may have struggled with some physical weakness. Paul tells him to "drink a little wine for the sake of your stomach because you are sick so often" (1 Tim. 5:23). While the cause of Timothy's stomachaches isn't shared, the church he led had many issues and it's not hard to imagine anxiety being a contributing factor. Paul reminds Timothy, "Physical training is good, but training for godliness is much better" (4:8). We often skip over the first part of the verse about physical training, but for those of us who struggle with anxiety, it's worth pausing to consider how good exercise is for us.

Psychiatrist John J. Ratey, who studies the effects of exercise on the brain, says, "A simple bike ride, dance class, or even a brisk walk can be a powerful tool for those suffering from chronic anxiety. Activities like these also help people who are feeling overly nervous and anxious about an upcoming test, a big presentation, or an important meeting."[1]

Ratey explains that exercise distracts us from what we're worried about, decreases muscle tension, changes our brain chemistry, helps control the fight-or-flight response, and increases resilience. What is the best kind and amount of exercise? Whatever you'll regularly do. Even a little can make a big difference.

We likely know how to exercise our bodies, but how do we do the same for our spiritual lives, as Paul encourages Timothy to do? One simple way that actually has similar benefits to physical exercise is meditation. Some of us have been taught that *meditate* is a scary word, but it actually just means intentionally thinking deeply or focusing. It's like a workout for your mind. The Psalms give us three areas that can work well for meditation:

- *God's love.* "We meditate on your unfailing love" (48:9).
- *God's ways and truth.* "I will meditate on your decrees" (119:23).
- *God's character and power.* "I will meditate on your majestic, glorious splendor and your wonderful miracles" (145:5).

Here's a basic meditation to try: Find a comfortable, quiet space to sit or lie down. Start a timer for five minutes. Then mentally repeat a Scripture such as, "For I can do everything through Christ, who gives me strength" (Phil. 4:13), and emphasize a different word each time. (I can do all things, I CAN do all things, I can DO all things). Take deep breaths in through your nose and out through your mouth while you do so.

Will your mind wander? Absolutely. When it does, gently, and without condemnation, bring it back. Every time you do this, it's like a bicep curl for your brain. Over time you will strengthen your ability to control your thoughts and therefore better manage your anxiety. Brain scans of those who meditate actually show physical differences over time.

The two things that set exercise apart from everyday movement and meditating from simply thinking are intentionality and consistency. If you exercise ten minutes a day and meditate for five, it's enough to have anxiety-reducing benefits.

Train your body.

Train your brain.

. . . .

God, you've made my body and mind in amazing ways. Help me to train both so I can fully use them to serve you and others. Amen.

Give it a try: Today, train your body for ten minutes (any type of movement counts) and meditate for five (if you haven't done this before, expect it to feel awkward). Write down your plan for when and how you'll do this in the future. If you need accountability to follow through, share your plan with someone.

FIFTY-FOUR

God Has Not Given You a Spirit of Fear

For God has not given us a spirit of fear and timidity, but of power, love, and self-discipline.

2 Timothy 1:7

Timothy holds the letter from Paul in his hands. He notices a splotch in the corner, perhaps a tear or remnants of the dampness of the Roman prison in which it was written. The two had been partnered in ministry for over fifteen years. They'd traveled together to Troas, Philippi, Corinth, and more places, sharing the gospel. Now Timothy leads a group of believers in the city of Ephesus—not an easy task.

Timothy grew up with a Jewish grandmother and mother, both of whom became believers. They taught him about Jesus, the Messiah, while his Greek father worshiped the gods. Paul became Timothy's spiritual

219

father and continual encourager. Now Timothy recognizes this will likely be Paul's last letter to him. In his first letter, Paul encourages Timothy to "fight the good fight for the true faith" (1 Tim. 6:12), but this time the tense is changed: "I have fought the good fight" (2 Tim. 4:7).

What does Paul want to impart to his son in the faith? *Courage.* "I remind you to fan into flames the spiritual gift God gave you when I laid my hands on you. For God has not given us a spirit of fear and timidity, but of power, love, and self-discipline" (1:6–7). These words are sometimes quoted as a rebuke, implying we should never be afraid. But Paul means them as the opposite—they are reassurance that no matter what's ahead, Timothy won't have to handle it on his own. We don't have to either.

Power. The original word is *dynamis*, and it's where we get the modern word *dynamic*. The power Paul speaks of is not human but supernatural. Fear tells us we are weak; God's Spirit makes us strong.

Love. This is *agape*, divine love. It's not what we see in romantic comedies. It's the fierce, wild love of God in and for us. Fear tells us to withdraw; God's Spirit empowers us to reach out.

Self-discipline. The word *sophronismos* can also be translated as "sound mind." It's an inner alignment with truth, a deep knowing that makes us brave. Fear tells us lies—we can't do it, we're not enough, we're going to fail; God's Spirit assures us we will prevail.

The temptation when we hear the words *power*, *love*, and *self-discipline* is to make them a personal checklist we have to accomplish on our own. When anxiety strikes, we tell ourselves to stop being afraid, get over it, push through, slap on a smile, and pretend we're fine. But we don't have to fake or force anything. We've been given a Spirit who lives within us and empowers us. We can turn Paul's words into an affirmation to repeat in anxious moments: "God has not given me a spirit of fear and timidity, but of power, love, and self-discipline."

Saying these words doesn't mean our fear will magically go away—Paul compares the life of faith to a fight, after all. But it will remind us that we, like Timothy, have everything we need to move forward in faith and finish strong.

....

God, thank you for giving me a spirit not of fear but of power, love, and self-discipline. I pray that you will empower me through your Spirit today. Amen.

When have you experienced the Spirit's power, love, and self-discipline in your life?

FIFTY-FIVE

God Empowers You to Run Your Race

Therefore, since we are surrounded by such a huge crowd of witnesses to the life of faith, let us strip off every weight that slows us down, especially the sin that so easily trips us up. And let us run with endurance the race God has set before us.

Hebrews 12:1

The unknown author of Hebrews likely would have heard the Greek story that led to the modern marathon. In 490 BC, the Persians landed at the city of Marathon on their way to attack Athens. A messenger named Pheidippides ran a significant distance to Sparta to request help. Running was also part of the early Olympic Games, and athletes truly did strip off every weight that slowed them down—they ran naked.

Thankfully, that practice has been discontinued, but athletes still pay attention to every ounce of weight in their equipment and clothing. Why? Every bit of weight takes energy because it has to be carried and that takes extra work. Obviously, the writer of Hebrews isn't talking about physical weight. So what weighs us down today? It turns out anxiety is one answer.

Researchers have mapped emotions on grids similar to this one:[1]

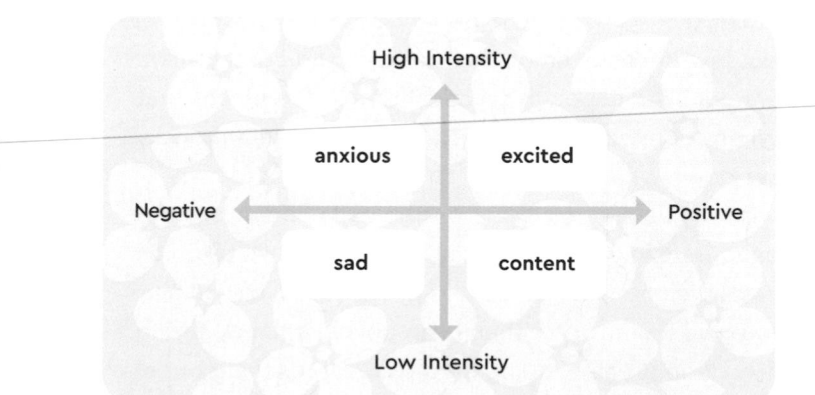

Negative, high-intensity emotions like anxiety are *heavy*. They stimulate your pituitary, hypothalamus, and adrenal glands, which release hormones related to your fight-or-flight response. These hormones might initially feel energizing, but they're not sustainable. And when they wear off, exhaustion takes their place.

When we live with consistent anxiety, we're also more likely to experience chronic fatigue. Our bodies carry a heavier load. It can seem like the solution would be to try to feel intense positive emotions instead, like excitement. Our culture also portrays emotions like this as the ultimate form of happiness. But even high-intensity positive emotions require extra energy.

For those of us who experience anxiety, positive but low-intensity emotions like calm and contentment are our sweet spot. In practical terms, this means that when we experience anxiety, we need to intentionally set down what's weighing on us and return to calm with the help of Jesus. For example, if I find myself caught up in worry, I can first notice that I've taken on extra weight. I can pause and pray, "Jesus, please help me give this to you." Then I can pursue calm by taking a few deep breaths, going for a walk, or reaching out to a friend. I may need to repeat this many times a day, and that's okay.

Ancient runners knew what our anxious hearts need to understand too. The ultimate goal of a race is progress, not perfection. It's perseverance, not a flawless performance. It's simply moving toward the finish line one step at a time.

....

God, you are the one who empowers me to run the race you have for me. Help me lay down anything that hinders me, like fear and anxiety. I will keep taking one step at a time toward the finish line. Amen.

What's weighing you down and using your energy? Pause and give it to Jesus now, and then take a practical step that helps too (remember, it's okay if you need to do so again throughout your day).

FIFTY-SIX

God Gets You through Stress to Joy

Consider it pure joy, my brothers and sisters, whenever you face trials of many kinds.

James 1:2 NIV

James thinks of his older half brother, memories of playing in front of their house, walking through the streets, sitting around their family's dinner table. Later his half brother turning water into wine, healing the sick, hanging on a cross, appearing to James after his resurrection. Why had it taken James so long to believe? Perhaps it's harder to recognize God when you're sharing dessert with him and he's sleeping in the same room as you.

It all made so much more sense now, especially how Jesus had the ability to see every problem that came his way as part of a bigger plan, even an opportunity for joy. He'd seen his half brother sad, angry, concerned, hurt but also happy, free, living with purpose and meaning. Now he wanted the same for his fellow Jewish believers. "Consider it pure joy, my brothers and sisters, whenever you face trials of many kinds" (James 1:2 NIV).

True confession: I don't like this verse, but lately I've been starting to think James is onto something. When psychologist and author Kelly McGonigal did in-depth research on stress, she reached a similar conclusion. She writes,

> When it came to overall well-being, the happiest people in the poll weren't the ones without stress. . . . I call this the *stress paradox*. High levels of stress are associated with both distress and well-being. Importantly, happy lives are not stress-free, nor does a stress-free life guarantee happiness. Even though most people view stress as harmful, higher levels of stress seem to go along with things we want: love, health, and satisfaction with our lives.[1]

Our teenage kids drive us crazy but also make us laugh.

Our spouse leaves laundry on the floor but cuddles with us on the couch.

Our job exasperates us at times but exhilarates us at others.

"Why are stress and meaning so strongly linked? One reason is that stress seems to be an inevitable consequence of engaging in roles and pursuing goals that feed our sense of purpose," says McGonigal.[2]

What about the stresses of life that are truly difficult, like illness, the death of a loved one, or losing our job? They may not make our lives feel more meaningful at the time, but they often prompt us to search for deeper meaning. I saw this during the early lockdown of the COVID-19 pandemic. No one would ever want a crisis like a pandemic to happen, but many people discovered surprising gifts in it, like reevaluated priorities, more time with family, or newfound gratitude for the simple things of life (like toilet paper).

When we struggle with anxiety, it can be easy to assume the answer is to make our lives stress-free. But James says, "You know that the testing of your faith produces perseverance. Let perseverance finish its work so that you may be mature and complete, not lacking anything" (James 1:3–4 NIV). It's easy to assume a stress-free life will lead to abundance. But if we eliminate everything that ever causes us any stress, it could actually mean the absence of things we long for—like relationships and growth.

Stress is uncomfortable, and we don't ever have to like it. But it can be helpful to see stress not as the enemy of joy but sometimes as a mysterious part of it.

. . . .

God, when life feels stressful, show me the hidden joy and meaning. Thank you for redeeming everything in my life, even stress, and using it all for my best. Amen.

What in your life stresses you out sometimes but also brings you joy?

FIFTY-SEVEN

God Transforms Being Anxious

You will be anxious to do the will of God.

1 Peter 4:2

Peter hears another report about Nero, the cruel emperor of Rome, persecuting Christians. He thinks of the new believers scattered throughout the places he's visited. How will they handle these difficulties, which will likely only get worse? He writes a letter to bolster their faith and shares an unexpected outcome of suffering: "You will be anxious to do the will of God" (1 Pet. 4:2).

This letter by Peter is one of the only times *anxious* appears in the New Testament, and it stands out because the word is used in a positive way. In this context, it's more like a synonym for excitement. Children are anxious for Christmas morning. Brides are anxious to walk down the aisle. An Olympic athlete who has diligently trained is anxious to finally compete.

It's easy to think of our anxiety as "all bad," but research has found it's actually closely related to excitement. "Anxiety and excitement are both aroused emotions. In both, the heart beats faster, cortisol surges, and the body prepares for action. . . . The only difference is that excitement is a positive emotion, focused on all the ways something could go well."[1] Anxiety and calm are opposites; anxiety and excitement are cousins.

What's the difference? Anxiety causes us to fixate on what we *don't* want. For early Christians, that was serious stuff, like persecution by an evil emperor. Excitement focuses on what we *do* want. For those same Christians, that was to do the will of God.

One technique that can help us shift from anxiety to excitement is asking ourselves, "What do I really want?" Anxiety for an Olympic athlete sounds like, "I don't want to fail." Excitement sounds like, "I want to do my absolute best." (Note that saying "I want to win a gold medal" isn't as helpful because we're not able to control factors influencing that outcome, like the performance of other athletes. Focus on what *you* can do.)

For us, anxiety-provoking situations are not likely to be as high-stakes as persecution or the Olympics. It's often the small, everyday concerns that trip us up most.

But this technique works for them too. In my life, anxiety before a social event often sounds like, "I don't want to say something awkward that will make people reject me." Excitement sounds more like, "I'm looking forward to connecting with old friends and maybe making new ones."

When we try to shift from anxiety to excitement, it might feel forced or fake—especially in the beginning. That's okay because researchers have found it works anyway. Have a good laugh about how awkward it sometimes feels to do this, and just keep going.

Let's be brave.

Let's be strong.

Let's be anxious to do the will of God.

....

God, when I'm anxious in a fear-based way, help me shift my perspective. I want to be anxious to do your will instead. Empower me to live differently today. Amen.

What's a time when you were excited about something? What did you think, feel, and do?

FIFTY-EIGHT

God Lets You Cast Your Cares on Him

Cast all your anxiety on him because he cares for you.

1 Peter 5:7 NIV

Peter thinks back to the moment when Jesus called him to be a disciple. "As Jesus walked beside the Sea of Galilee, he saw Simon and his brother Andrew casting a net into the lake, for they were fishermen" (Mark 1:16 NIV). That word, *casting*, had been such a part of his everyday life. Jesus turned him into a fisher of people, and as he writes, that same word comes back to him again.

To understand what "cast all your anxiety on him" (1 Pet. 5:7 NIV) really means, we need to understand how fishing worked in biblical times. A fisherman like Peter would have had a personal cast net about eight to fifteen feet in diameter. Attached to the center of this net would have been a line, which the fisherman held in his left hand. Then he would have hurled the net toward the sea with his right hand. The net would have spread wide, landed on the water, then fallen like a parachute, capturing all the fish below.

When Peter invites us to cast our cares on God, it's permission to free our hearts of them. I think of this as I stand at the edge of a pond, ripples across the waters mirroring those of my unsettled heart. I pick up a rock the size of my palm and place it in my hand, running my fingers across the surface worn smooth by time and troubles.

I bend over, pull my elbow back as if I'm a human slingshot, and throw the stone. It flies over the midnight-blue surface before skipping once, twice, and disappearing from view. I wipe the dust off my hands.

Sometimes we put pressure on ourselves to just "give it to God" and then feel like spiritual failures when our worries come back again. But Peter would have known this is part of the process. He didn't just cast his net once; he did it over and over again. We may need to do the same. Peter also knew that when you cast a net, it sometimes comes back empty. But God doesn't leave us with emptiness when we let him have our cares. He gives us peace, grace, strength, and whatever else we need.

Releasing our cares isn't a onetime event. It's a life-long process. We can come to the shore of God's faithful love again and again, as often as we need. Yes, we are always welcome to give him whatever weighs us down so that we can continue our journey with freer, lighter hearts.

To cast our cares means more than just a tentative letting go—it's a hurling, tossing, complete release. This is the offer of God: to let him take our anxieties as the lake takes our stones, fully and completely. There is enough room to hold one care or a thousand. We can let them all sink beneath the surface of his endlessly deep love.

....

God, I'm grateful for the invitation to cast my cares on you. None of them are too big or too small. Help me release them all to you. Amen.

What care do you need to release to God today? What does he want to give you instead?

FIFTY-NINE

God's Love for You Is Perfect

There is no fear in love. But perfect love drives out fear, because fear has to do with punishment. The one who fears is not made perfect in love.

1 John 4:18 NIV

Hey, Son of Thunder!" John turns to see Peter walking toward him, a grin on his face. When Jesus called John and his brother James to follow him, they left their father's fishing boat immediately. Jesus gave them this nickname, and Peter hasn't forgotten.

Why Sons of Thunder? Perhaps their father thundered after them, telling them to, as many parents do, "Get back here right now!" Maybe James and John had fierce tempers. (They did once ask Jesus if he wanted them to call down fire from heaven on people. Um, no.) Or the name could have been inspired by their ambitious mama, who asked Jesus for her sons to sit at the right and left hand of Jesus in heaven (um, no again).

Scripture doesn't explain the meaning of the nickname, but we do know John eventually trades it for another—"the disciple Jesus loved." This phrase is used five times in the Gospel of John. The first time it appears is at the Last Supper, just after Jesus washes the feet of his disciples. Imagine John, with his fiery family, temper, or legacy of ambition, watching his leader kneel before him to do the work of a servant. It appears to be a transformational aha moment for John, one where he realizes his true identity is simply this: *beloved*.

Toward the end of John's life, this remains true as he writes, "There is no fear in love. But perfect love drives out fear, because fear has to do with punishment. The one who fears is not made perfect in love" (1 John 4:18 NIV). The true meaning of the word *perfect* in the Bible is different from how we often think of it. It's about wholeness and completion. John is saying that when we fully know we're loved, we're no longer afraid.

We don't often associate anger or ambition with anxiety, but the two are actually closely related. Fear triggers our fight-or-flight response, and anger is the fight reaction. Ambition can be a flight reaction when we run from our insecurity by pursuing accomplishments.

John says instead we can "know and rely on the love God has for us" (v. 16 NIV). I've written my own versions of this, and I imagine you have too. I know and rely on the power of brownies to make me feel better. I know and rely on the comfort of a good ole pity party. I know and rely on my ability to keep trying harder until I prove my worth. Amen? God doesn't condemn us for this; he loves us completely and as is. But he does whisper to our hearts, "I have something better for you."

When we're anxious, we can ask ourselves, "What's one thing I can do that will help me know and rely on God's love for me?" We might tell a trustworthy friend or counselor we're not okay, and let them speak encouragement to us. We may go for a walk in nature so we can see how God cares for the birds, the flowers, and us. We could pause to pray, listen to music that calms us, or embrace the gift of rest through a much-needed nap. What we choose doesn't have to be "religious"—it only needs to reveal more of God's love in our lives.

John discovered a heart-freeing truth we can embrace today. Even in our anxious, angry, or ambitious moments, two things never change: God's love and our true identity. We are fully and always beloved.

....

God, help me know and rely on the love you have for me today. Open my eyes to see your love everywhere. Open my ears to hear it wherever I go. Open my hands and heart to fully receive it. I want to live as your beloved. Amen.

What are three ways you can rely on God's love when you're anxious? Refer back to the ideas in today's reading if needed.

SIXTY

God Will Set You Free from Anxiety

> He will wipe every tear from their eyes, and there will be no more death or sorrow or crying or pain. All these things are gone forever.
>
> Revelation 21:4

John walks along the shore of Patmos, a tiny Greek island in the Aegean Sea where he was exiled for preaching the gospel in Asia. Compared to the Roman prison Paul endured, Patmos seems like a paradise. A travel journalist describes a section called Rainbow Beach: "The beach here is dotted with small, multi-colored pebbles ranging from butterscotch orange to sweet potato red and egg yolk yellow—and the combined effect is extraordinary."[1]

It's in this context that God reveals wonders to John as if to say, "You think this beach is beautiful? Wait until you see what's still to come." John writes, "The one sitting on the throne was as brilliant as gemstones—like jasper and carnelian. And the glow of an emerald circled his throne like a rainbow" (Rev. 4:3). Even more than what we can see, John helps us look forward to what will finally happen to all our hurts and struggles in eternity. "God himself will be with them. He will wipe every tear from their eyes, and there will be no more death or sorrow or crying or pain. All these things are gone forever" (21:3–4).

This moment when God wipes all the tears from our eyes will also be the end of our anxiety. We will never again experience fear. We won't worry, doubt, or second-guess ourselves. We'll live with complete peace, joy, and love. We catch glimpses of that in this life, perhaps when we're laughing with friends on a summer evening, watching a bride walk down the aisle, holding a baby in our arms, creating art that lights us up inside, watching a bird soar or a dolphin swim. They're moments when we have no self-consciousness, when we're caught up in something bigger and wilder than we are, when the critical voice inside us goes silent in awe. We're no longer anxious; we're fully absorbed in the moment.

In heaven, we will live like this always. John doesn't say we'll stand around singing forever (so you can stop feeling bad if you thought that actually sounded pretty boring). We'll first sit down to a feast, to a grand celebration. We'll meet Jesus face-to-face. We'll reconnect with people we love. We'll fully become who we were created to be all along. All our anxiety will finally be gone. Close your eyes and imagine it for a moment.

Between now and then, we're all just on a journey Home. I pray our time together the last sixty days has given you hope and new tools that will help you along the way. But I also want to whisper, "This is only the beginning." God has so much more for you, in this life and in eternity. Until then, remember that you are God's beloved. You are never alone. Your anxiety can't defeat or define you because you already know the final chapter of the story. Love, not anxiety, overcomes in the end.

....

God, thank you for the journey I'm on with you. I look forward to the joyful day when I'm forever free of anxiety. Until then, I will keep moving forward one step at a time with you. Amen.

What's a truth you want to remember from this book?

YOUR NEXT STEP

For more encouragement and resources to help
you continue to walk in freedom from anxiety, go to
www.holleygerth.com/anxiety.

ACKNOWLEDGMENTS

To my editor, Jennifer Leep, thank you for more than a decade of doing books together. You're not only the person whose perspective makes everything I write better, but you're also a dear and trusted friend.

To my wonderful team at Revell—especially Wendy Wetzel, Amy Ballor, and Kelli Smith—I'm so grateful for the years we've spent together, and I look forward to what's ahead.

To my virtual assistant, Kaitlyn Bouchillon, your diligence, excellence, creativity, and friendship help more than you could ever know. I appreciate all you do.

To my business partner, Jason Rovenstine, your kindness, brilliance, and encouragement inspire me. Thanks for making what I do and who I am better.

To Mom and Dad, thanks for teaching me that love is powerful and kindness is courageous, and for praying for me through every adventure. And, Mom, thank you for listening to me read every word of this book to you! You made it so much stronger.

To my grandmother, Eula Armstrong, you are an example of resilience and following Jesus for a lifetime. Thank you for all your prayers.

To my daughter, Lovelle, you're a gift, and God knew exactly what our family needed—brave, bright-shining, joy-bringing, beautiful you!

To my grandkids, Eula and Clement, I can't wait to see who God created you to be. You're already a delight.

To my husband, Mark, there are hardly enough words to describe all you are to me. Partner, friend, encourager, and the man I will be in love with all my life. I'm thankful every day to share this adventure with you.

To my local and faraway friends, thanks for being cheerleaders, advisers, and prayer warriors while I wrote this book.

To all my readers, thank you for helping shape this book through all the wisdom you offered, insights you gave, and stories you shared.

Most of all, to God, thank you for your faithful love that sees me through whatever I face. Nothing is impossible with you.

NOTES

Introduction

1. "New APA Poll Shows Surge in Anxiety Among Americans Top Causes Are Safety, COVID-19, Health, Gun Violence, and the Upcoming Election," American Psychiatric Association, October 21, 2020, www.psychiatry.org /newsroom/news-releases/anxiety-poll-2020.

Chapter 1 God Will Meet You Where You Are Today

1. *Lexico*, s.v., "anxiety," accessed December 9, 2021, https://www.lexico .com/en/definition/anxiety.

2. Brené Brown, *The Gifts of Imperfection: Let Go of Who You Think You're Supposed to Be and Embrace Who You Are* (Center City, MN: Hazelden Publishing, 2010), 9–10.

Chapter 6 God Gives You a New Song

1. Yana Hoffman and Hank Davis, "Sing in the Shower to Make Friends with Your Vagus Nerve," *Psychology Today*, March 17, 2020, https://www .psychologytoday.com/us/blog/try-see-it-my-way/202003/sing-in-the -shower-make-friends-your-vagus-nerve.

Chapter 14 God Speaks to You in the Storm

1. *Forrest Gump*, directed by Robert Zemeckis (1994; Hollywood, CA: Paramount Pictures, 2001), DVD.

Chapter 15 God Is Your Good Shepherd

1. W. Phillip Keller, *A Shepherd Looks at Psalm 23* (Grand Rapids: Zondervan, 2007), 97.

2. Keller, *A Shepherd*, 102.

Chapter 20 God Is Greater Than All Your Fears

1. Chuck Swindoll, "Proverbs," Insight for Living Ministries, accessed December 15, 2021, www.insight.org/resources/bible/the-wisdom-books /proverbs.

2. William D. Eisenhower, "Fearing God," *Christianity Today*, February 7, 1986, https://www.christianitytoday.com/ct/1986/february-7/fearing-god -those-who-have-never-trembled-from-head-to-toe.html.

Chapter 21 God Alone Knows Your Future

1. Eva M. Krockow, "How Many Decisions Do We Make Each Day?" *Psychology Today*, September 27, 2018, https://www.psychologytoday.com/us /blog/stretching-theory/201809/how-many-decisions-do-we-make-each-day.

Chapter 22 God Is in Your Everyday Moments

1. University of Vermont Medical Center, "Mindful Monday: Try the 'Five Senses' Mindfulness Exercise," UVM Medical Center Blog, January 29, 2019, https://medcenterblog.uvmhealth.org/wellness/physical/mindfulness-mindful -monday-exercise/.

Chapter 26 God Is Calling You

1. Daniel Goleman, *Social Intelligence: The Revolutionary New Science of Human Relationships* (New York: Random House, 2006), 4.

Chapter 27 God Is Your Ultimate Certainty

1. Jonathan Fields, *Uncertainty: Turning Fear and Doubt into Fuel for Brilliance* (New York: Portfolio, 2012), chap. 4, Kindle.

Chapter 29 God Will Bring New Life and Growth

1. Adam Grant, "There's a Name for the Blah You're Feeling: It's Called Languishing," *New York Times*, April 19, 2021, https://www.nytimes.com/2021/04 /19/well/mind/covid-mental-health-languishing.html.

2. Grant, "There's a Name for the Blah."

Chapter 31 God Is Your Caretaker

1. Alison Escalante, "New Science: Why Our Brains Spend 50 Percent of the Time Mind-Wandering," *Forbes*, January 28, 2021, www.forbes.com/sites /alisonescalante/2021/01/28/new-science-why-our-brains-spend-50-of-the -time-mind-wandering/?sh=24803e04854e.

2. Escalante, "New Science."

Chapter 34 God Lets You Draw Near

1. "Clean, Unclean," *Baker's Evangelical Dictionary of Biblical Theology*, Biblestudytools.com, accessed December 16, 2021, www.biblestudytools.com/dictionaries/bakers-evangelical-dictionary/clean-unclean.html.

Chapter 41 God Will Renew Your Mind

1. Martin Lindstrom, "Why Fear Sells: The Business of Panic and Paranoia," Brain World, November 23, 2019, https://brainworldmagazine.com/fear-sells-business-panic-paranoia/.

Chapter 42 God Shows Up in Your Awkward Moments

1. A. Pawlowski, "Feel Red Cheeks Coming On? Nine Ways to Overcome Blushing," *Today*, September 22, 2016, https://www.today.com/health/feel-red-cheeks-coming-9–ways-overcome-blushing-t103164.

2. Pawlowski, "Feel Red Cheeks."

3. Pawlowski, "Feel Red Cheeks."

Chapter 43 God Clears the Clutter in Your Life

1. Anne-Marie Gambelin, "It's Science: Clutter Can Actually Give You Anxiety," Motherly, January 11, 2018, https://www.mother.ly/life/its-science-clutter-can-actually-give-you-anxiety.

2. Gretchen Rubin, *Outer Order, Inner Calm: Declutter and Organize to Make Room for Happiness* (New York: Harmony Books, 2019), xii–xiii.

Chapter 47 God Will Help You Fight for Peace

1. John McRay, "Stench, Pain, and Misery," *Christianity Today*, July 01, 1995, https://www.christianitytoday.com/history/issues/issue-47/stench-pain-and-misery.html.

Chapter 48 God Will Help You Retrain Your Brain

1. Amy Palmer, "The Neuroscience of Visualization," *Mind Movies Blog*, accessed December 18, 2021, www.mindmovies.com/blogroll/the-neuroscience-of-visualization.

Chapter 49 God Equips You to Handle Anything

1. *Old and New Testament Greek Lexical Dictionary*, s.v. "Strong's #842," accessed January 4, 2022, https://www.studylight.org/lexicons/eng/greek/842.html.

2. Susan Jeffers, PhD, *Feel the Fear and Do It Anyway: Dynamic Techniques for Turning Fear, Indecision, and Anger into Power, Action, and Love* (Santa Monica, CA: Jeffers Press, 2007), chap. 1, Kindle.

Chapter 50 God Can Even Use Conflict

1. David Johnson and Jeff VanVonderen, *The Subtle Power of Spiritual Abuse* (Bloomington, MN: Bethany House, 2005), 90.

Chapter 51 God Connects with You in Creative Ways

1. Gary Thomas, *Sacred Pathways: Nine Ways to Connect with God* (Grand Rapids: Zondervan, 2020).

Chapter 53 God Is the Ultimate Trainer

1. John J. Ratey, "Can Exercise Help Treat Anxiety?" Harvard Health Publishing, October 24, 2019, https://www.health.harvard.edu/blog/can-exercise-help-treat-anxiety-2019102418096.

Chapter 55 God Empowers You to Run Your Race

1. Adapted from Emma Seppala, *The Happiness Track: How to Apply the Science of Happiness to Accelerate Your Success* (San Francisco: HarperOne, 2016), chap. 3, Kindle.

Chapter 56 God Gets You through Stress to Joy

1. Kelly McGonigal, *The Upside of Stress: Why Stress Is Good for You, and How to Get Good at It* (New York: Penguin, 2016), 64.

2. McGonigal, *The Upside*, 65.

Chapter 57 God Transforms Being Anxious

1. Olga Khazan, "Can Three Words Turn Anxiety into Success?" *The Atlantic*, March 23, 2016, https://www.theatlantic.com/health/archive/2016/03/can-three-words-turn-anxiety-into-success/474909/.

Chapter 60 God Will Set You Free from Anxiety

1. John Malathronas, "Patmos: The Greek Island Where the End of the World Began," CNN, September 28, 2018, https://www.cnn.com/travel/article/patmos-island-greece/index.html.

ABOUT HOLLEY

HOLLEY GERTH loves humans, words, and good coffee. She's a *Wall Street Journal* bestselling author, life coach, and, as well as a cofounder of The Potentialist Agency. Holley cofounded the groundbreaking online community (in)courage, which had almost one million page views in its first six months, and cohosts the *More Than Small Talk* podcast. Holley is also wife to Mark, mom to Lovelle, and Nana to Eula and Clement. Connect with her and sign up for free encouraging emails from her at holleygerth.com.

Connect with
HOLLEY

HolleyGerth.com

@HolleyGerth

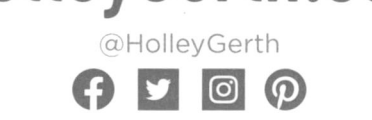

60 TRUTH-FILLED DEVOTIONS FOR THOSE IN NEED OF PEACE

This encouraging devotional from Holley Gerth offers spiritual truth to soothe your soul and practical tools to apply that will truly make a difference. Each day, Holley offers Scripture, a prayer, questions for reflection, and inspirational quotes to help you learn to live with more calm and less chaos, more worship and less worry.

ENCOURAGEMENT TO LIVE AS A WOMAN OF CONFIDENCE AND VICTORY

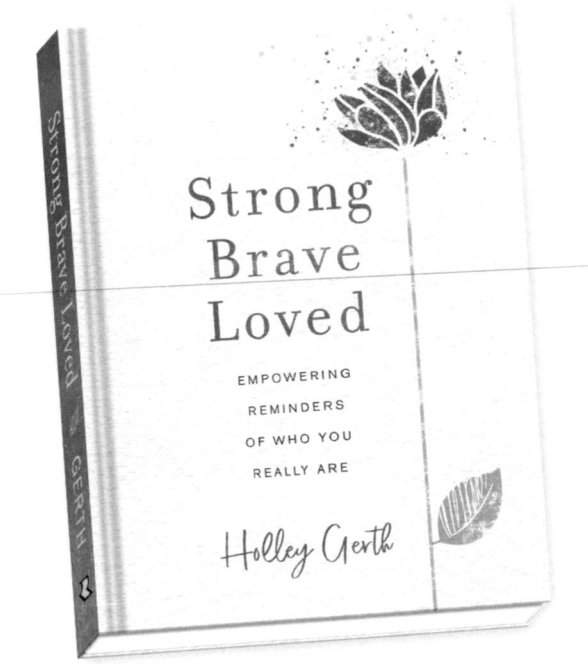

Holley Gerth offers you sixty short devotions to empower you to be a woman who fights to believe she is who God says she is and helps others do the same.

FIND ENCOURAGEMENT FROM GOD'S PROMISES TO FACE EACH DAY

In this uplifting book, Holley Gerth invites you to be filled with the strength, peace, and joy that come from God's promises. Each of the fifty-two devotions based on the Psalms will help you remember that God is good and we're all in this together.